"'Jesus is not as concerned with what we do, but who we are.' This is a precious pearl of truth that Dr. Mark Peters holds up to the light in his new book, *If You Die Today! Where Will You Be Tomorrow?*

Dr. Peters employs a format similar to his previous two books, wherein he bases each of the 11 chapters upon a singular element of the title, be it word or punctuation mark. These individual elements provide a springboard for diving deep into the different components of the title question.

What especially struck me about the way Mark brought answers to the surface, was how he attached a beatitude to each one and allowed the teaching of Jesus to float it up to the top. Thus, each chapter builds upon the preceding chapter in much the same way that the beatitudes build upon each other. This really depicts the transformative progression that occurs when one is drawn to Christ by God's grace, dies to self, and is nourished by faith in Christ to produce spiritual fruit. This is the kind of fruit that is good today, will be good tomorrow, and lasts forever.

Thanks again, Mark, for not only being a *hearer* of the word but a *doer* who encourages others by your candidness, transparency, and steadfast commitment to the Word of God and the love of Jesus Christ!"

—Mr. Bob Leffingwell

"Fantastic book! Best of the three that Mark has written! Drives home the point that we let our busy lives keep us from spending time with our Lord and Savior. The pivotal question we all must face is in the title: *If You Die Today! Where Will You Be Tomorrow?*"

—Dr. Buddy McClung

"The eternity of man is at stake, and the solution is the gospel *for it is the power of God for salvation.* How will we respond to a world that desperately needs to hear this message? Mark unashamedly proclaims the good news of the gospel and shares his life experiences of living this out. His stories are captivating, his exhortation for believers to deepen their faith is unfeigned, and his passion for sharing Christ is encouraging. The question of one's eternity is paramount and as I read this book it challenged me to think about how I should be sharing the gospel with the people who God has put in my life."

—Mr. Jon Helander

"This book reflects a dogged persistence and perseverance in sharing the gospel with others.

Through these pages, the reader is shown examples of how we believers could all more consistently live our lives each day for our Lord Jesus Christ. As well, the book gives a glimpse into the life purpose of a simple God-fearing Christian who wants to make a difference for our Lord by impacting those around him into thinking about who, or Who it is that they are actually worshiping.

Mark has applied these principles of persistence and perseverance to his life's purpose of sharing with others the gift of eternal life through Jesus Christ. Through the pages of this book, the reader sees and feels the love that Mark has for all people. Just as Jesus does, Mark wants all of us to have this wonderful gift of eternal life. I can attest that this is the 'real deal.'"

—John E. Leland, DDS

"For those of you who have read Mark's first two books, or know him personally, he is anything but timid to get personal and ask people questions no one has probably asked them before. In this book, he is asking the most important question anyone could ever ask or be asked, "If you die today, where will you be tomorrow?" He confronts all of us to seriously consider our answer to that question because what we believe matters for all our eternity. He asks us if we are willing to trust in the truths of God and Jesus Christ, which lead to eternal life, peace, and joy, or the lies of Satan and the world, which lead to eternal separation from God and torment in hell.

Mark has a passion for those who have never considered their relationship with God and Jesus Christ and those who profess to be Christian but live no differently than the world around them. He asks us to look at how we spend our time, obtaining more stuff, which never satisfies, or pursuing a relationship with our Creator that will give lasting peace and joy. This book helps us examine our heart attitudes about which tomorrow we are living for, the one that leads to eternal life and fulfillment through Jesus Christ or the one that pursues the things of this world that never satisfy and lead to eternal death. You will find it helpful in giving you questions . . . and answers as to why you are living your life."

—Dr. Steve Dwyer

"This book helps reveal the connection of God's Word to our daily lives in relation to the most important question we could ever be asked this side of eternity. It helps us to peer into the Beatitudes and how they, when understood, help us to see ourselves in the light of God's righteous and perfect standard. Mark has beautifully shined a light onto the great thing in life so often ignored in our culture—a daily relationship with Jesus Christ our Lord. I recommend diving in!"

—Dr. Joe McCollum

IF YOU DIE

TODAY!

WHERE WILL YOU BE TOMORROW?

MARK PETERS

LUCIDBOOKS

I thank my Lord Jesus Christ for His patience, mercy, grace, and love that He has rained down on me—a sinner.

I'm thankful for my amazing wife, Keyea— who I absolutely don't deserve.

I'm thankful for my daughter Kailey, her husband Dustin, and our son Joseph—all of whom continue to humble me with their maturity in their walks of faith at an age when I was running away from God.

I'm thankful for Kynlee Joy—my granddaughter who is coming soon!

CONTENTS

PREFACE

R ecently, my wife, Keyea, and I were having dinner at our favorite "date" restaurant through these past 35 years. She asked me, "Well, how is the book coming?"

"It seems to be coming along nicely. It amazes me at how the Lord brings all of this together each time I've written one of my books."

"How so?" she inquired.

"The structure of this book is a little different, but in many ways similar to the other two. All three books ended up with the same number of chapters: 11. All three have one-word titles for each chapter, as well as a question mark and exclamation point to head up two of the chapters."

She gave me a querying eye and asked, "Didn't you plan it that way?"

"Not really, it just worked out this way. I think it was the Lord's intention for it to do so," I stated.

"Hmmm," she said, still pondering my statement.

A conscious decision . . .

One thing you will notice about all three of these books is the different fonts used throughout them. Here is the reason, as I explained it to one of the editors. The editor of my second book had advised me to use the same font and print for the Scriptures as I had for the rest of the text of the manuscript I had sent him.

"It looks cleaner and neater," he had said, and I can certainly understand his recommendation. I mentioned to him that there was a method to my madness in that the people reading these books may have never read much, if any, from a Bible before. I wanted there to be no mistake on who, or Who, wrote what. I wanted clarity that what the Holy Word of God said and what I said in my feeble commentary on it—were clearly understood and delineated. To those new to reading God's Word, there can be trepidation and intimidation as to what it says and means to them in their lives. You will find a lot of Scripture from the Bible in this book and I would ask you to trust me and read through it, even if there are times you may find yourself a little challenged by what it says. The Lord blesses those who read His Word and there is much power in all of us reading it.

Also, all Scripture references in this book are from the New American Standard Bible (NASB). There are many different versions that the Bible is written in. I have mainly used the Revised Standard Version (RSV), the New International Version (NIV), or the New American Standard Bible (NASB) in my 34 years of Bible study. God's Word is living and active to each of us who read it:

For the word of God is living and active and sharper than any two-edged sword, and piercing as far as the division of soul and spirit, of both joints and marrow, and able to judge the thoughts and intentions of the heart. And there is no creature hidden from His sight, but all things are open and laid bare to the eyes of Him with whom we have to do.

Heb. 4:12–13

The last thing I would ever want to do would be to misrepresent our Lord and Savior or His infallible, unerring, and truthful Word! I don't take lightly what the Lord has, in my understanding, compelled me to do in writing three books on the Christian faith that I never had any intention of writing. Friends, I am a dentist! And, I am a knucklehead, scumbag sinner who was merrily on my way to an eternity in hell before my Lord grabbed me by the scruff of my neck at a Christian concert when I was 28 years old! Jesus Christ had a grip on me that I couldn't shake free from—and today, I am so humbly, meekly, and tearfully thankful that my Lord loves me, shows His grace and mercy to me, and has redeemed me for eternity through His death on the cross, and subsequent resurrection from the dead—which enables me to join Him and His Father in heaven one day! Praise Jesus Christ's Holy name!

Another insight for you to consider as you read this book, is that I have quoted—sometimes extensively—from others I consider to be giants in the faith. Besides spending time in His Word each day, the Lord has given me a desire to read a lot of the works of people whose strong faith is evidenced in their lives and writings that the Lord has had them do. Rather than me trying to paraphrase and lose some of the verve that they have in their message, I felt the need to let their words speak to you, as they certainly have to me. Also, I have included a reading list in the back of this book which contains some of the books that are cited, as well as others that I've read that might help in giving insight to those wanting to look into what it is that they truly believe.

I pray that Jesus will bring all of those He calls to faith in Him and do it all for His own glory! Jesus Christ alone deserves the glory because it has all been accomplished by Him and Him alone! Jesus Christ is my Lord and I am not ashamed of Him or His gospel. May He use this poor effort at sharing His truth to accomplish what He wills for it to do!

INTRODUCTION

L aura, my editor, asked me what the purpose of this book was. The funny thing was—she asked it after she had read the entire manuscript!

The purpose of this book is to help people of all faiths or of no faith—to "think." I have visited with many people through the years about what they believe regarding whatever faith they are clinging to. A common trait of most that I have visited with seems to be that they are not sure what it is that they truly believe—they don't really think about it that much. Life is busy!

This is a huge problem if there is an eternity in each of our future. If there is an eternal existence for us, we should want to be sure of where we end up for that eternity. Right?

Also, many of the Christian faith seem to be in much the same boat—many do not know what they truly believe regarding the gospel and how they will end up in heaven.

We all are seeking different things in this short life, so we can live it to the fullest. Visiting with others seeking happiness in this world has shown me that many are having a difficult time in knowing where to look for that happiness.

Jesus longs for us to long for Him, but why are we not doing so? Christ has given me a passion for spending time hungering and thirsting for His righteousness and encouraging others around me to do the same. Seeking a close and personal, intimate relationship with Christ is the only endeavor that will fill us with joy and bring us true happiness this side of heaven! The question is, "Why are so few Christians doing so while they are living this life God Himself has given them?"

This book will delve into this topic in ways that my other two books didn't. The world and Satan have a tight hold on many, if not most, of those who are on the planet right now. What are the many doing to seek the joy and happiness that the world tells them is just beyond their fingertips? Unfortunately, most are seeking it from sources which can never oblige them on their elusive quest!

Will you and I be honest enough with ourselves that we will acknowledge that all the stuff we accumulate does not ever bring the contentment we seem to be seeking. True joy can only come from the Lord who pursues us while we run from Him and seek our own selfish wills. It is time for us to die to ourselves and be emptied of ourselves in order to be filled with the Holy Spirit our Lord is only too happy to provide—if we will repent, humble ourselves, and avail ourselves to Him.

Come along with me as we explore what it means to hunger and thirst for Christ's righteousness. Whether you consider yourself a Christian or aren't sure what to think about it all, this is book is for you. You will find some answers to questions you may never have even thought about asking—because you may find yourself starting to "think!"

CHAPTER 1

IF

If anyone has ears to hear, let him hear.

Mark 7:16

"If" is a thinking person's word. It denotes a decision or possibility that may exist in the upcoming future of a moment, a day, a life, or an eternity. There are however two "ifs" that impact us in this physical life we are each living that we cannot get away from, and we will be discovering what they both are at the start of our time together.

An Opportunity That Would Have Been Missed Before . . .

Her name was Sandy, and she had come to the office to do another physical exam. I had given her a copy of my book, *Which Way Is Up?*[1] about three or four years earlier. I hadn't seen her since and probably wouldn't see her again, unless I needed to do another physical for insurance purposes. She volunteered that she hadn't read any of the book, but when I brought up the title of my second book, *Christian Family MELTDOWN!*, she said, "Now that is a book I would read! My family has had all kinds of problems over these Christmas holidays."

That was my in, so I asked her, "What kind of problems, Sandy?"

She shared, "Oh, you know . . . the same kind of problems most families have when feelings get hurt and emotions are at a high, in the frenzy of getting through Christmas."

That led to my statement: "It is a shame that we often forget the true meaning of Christmas, and let the commercialism of the world take over what a truly holy day it really is."

"Yes, it is," she countered.

"Do you go to church anywhere, Sandy?"

"Oh, I've been to and visited various churches over the years, but frankly I haven't found one I would feel comfortable staying in. I mean, look, the last church I visited was one I went to with a friend of mine, and it just didn't seem genuine to me."

"Full of hypocrites, huh?" I quipped.

"Yeah, how did you know? There I was sitting with my friend, who's a drunk all week long, listening to her carry on about how wonderful her walk of faith is, and then talking bad about the other people at her church that she knew. It really turned me off."

"I know what you mean, Sandy. I've heard that comment so many times. You know the problem? The problem is that in reality, all of us are hypocrites! When I hear someone complaining about hypocrites in the church, I try to let them know that they are right, because all of us are hypocrites. In fact, I tell them that they should come on in and join us, because they are hypocrites as well, if they will truly look at themselves."

She laughed and said, "Yeah, I guess you're right about that."

It was then that I asked her the question that I've asked so many people through the years: "Sandy, if you die today, where will you be tomorrow?"

Her response was one of the most common that I usually hear: "Well, I would hope I would be in heaven!"

"Don't we all!" I replied. "OK, can I ask you another question?"

"Sure."

"Why would you be there?"

"Well, I'm a good person! I haven't killed anybody or anything like that, and I'm better than most of the people out there!"

"Sandy, that's a response I have heard so many times from others as well. But I've got some thoughts for you to consider if you will. Can I share them with you? That is, if you've got a few minutes?"

"Yeah, I'm in no rush. What are they?"

"Well, I think many people are misled and not sure of what they exactly believe in. Many that I've asked those questions to have responded almost exactly as you just did. That is what concerns me with people who respond that way. If you and they are thinking that being a good person is going to get you to heaven, there's a possibility that you, like others who feel the same way, could be on the wrong path. This path could maybe end up with you spending eternity where you don't want to spend it. And eternity is a long, long time!"

She looked back at me with eyes that told me how much she was seriously considering my words. We will get back to this encounter later in this chapter.

The Answer . . .

If I am still alive, will you not show me the lovingkindness of the LORD, that I may not die?

1 Sam. 20:14

Lovingkindness, that's what we need. That's the ticket. We need a God who will love us and show us that love all the time in every way. Our problem is that we want to worship the god we want him to be rather than the God He really is. We want to take God to task and make Him out to be what we think He should be, not trust that He is the Omnipotent and Omnipresent God Almighty of the universe. Yes, He loves us, and yes, He provides for us; but He is perfectly holy—and without one flaw. Because He is perfectly holy, God cannot allow sin to be masked, left in our lives, and unjudged. God's standard of perfect and holy righteousness is the one and only standard that will be used in determining who will, or won't, be in heaven.

The Holy God of the universe wants us to be Holy as well. Our God wants us to worship Him the way that He wants us to worship Him—in relationship with Him and dependent on Him. He doesn't give us license to put Him in a box and morph Him into what we, as sinners, want Him to be. Our culture has invaded the church much more seemingly than our churches have made inroads into our culture. It is evident everywhere! This results in many who attend our churches being at a misrepresented and misinformed state as to their salvation in Christ. The deception of the "fallen one," the "father of lies," is rampant, and he is vigilant in misleading many who think they are at a good place in relationship to our Lord.

The Lord has put it on my heart to show His lovingkindness to those around me so that they may not be misguided. And no, I don't have all the answers, nor do I have a lock on wisdom—in fact, far from it. I am a knucklehead sinner just like the rest of mankind! Our Lord has given me my salvation through His grace, His dying on the cross, and His being resurrected to save me from my sins. I am now redeemed from my sins

and reconciled to Him, the Father, and the Holy Spirit. Jesus
has shown so much love to me that I feel compelled to show
His love to those in whose hands He puts this book. Jesus also
speaks of us believers sharing His truth:

> But now I come to You; and these things I speak in
> the world so that they may have My joy made full in
> themselves. I have given them Your word; and the
> world has hated them, because they are not of the
> world, even as I am not of the world. I do not ask You
> to take them out of the world, but to keep them from
> the evil one. They are not of the world, even as I am not
> of the world. Sanctify them in the truth; Your word is
> truth. As You sent Me into the world, I also have sent
> them into the world. For their sakes I sanctify Myself,
> that they themselves also may be sanctified in truth. I
> do not ask on behalf of these alone, but for those also
> who believe in Me through their word; that they may all
> be one; even as You, Father, are in Me and I in You, that
> they also may be in Us, so that the world may believe
> that You sent Me.
>
> **John 17:13–21**

I do realize, however, that there are those who don't believe
God's Bible is true and they will take exception to the previous
verses. But still, shouldn't we, who are believers in Christ, warn
those around us in an effort to help their eyes to be opened to
what we have learned? After all, I can attest that my beliefs are
diametrically opposed from where they were in my younger
years. My eyes were closed to the Lord Jesus Christ, but they
are not so anymore. So, I will continue to share the life of Jesus
Christ with those around me and those who may read this
book.

> **Yet if you have warned the wicked and he does not turn**
> **from his wickedness or from his wicked way, he shall**
> **die in his iniquity; but you have delivered yourself.**
> **Ezek. 3:19**

This book is written as a help and warning to all who read it. It speaks to the fact that what we do MATTERS! What we say MATTERS! And what or Who we believe in for our redemption for eternity—MATTERS!

The Lie . . .

Satan is a liar and the "father of lies" (John 8:44)! And he wants you and me in hell with him and not in heaven. In fact, he sees this as one of his highest priorities—to thwart and deceive all those he can into believing in the wrong things, so they are lost to an eternity of separation from God, along with eternal misery in hell. And based on the spiraling down of the world around us, he is doing an excellent job at carrying out that quest.

What about you? Has he got you deceived into believing his lies? Many, if not most, do not know what the TRUTH really is. Our world and Satan would have us believe that there is no TRUTH. If there is no TRUTH, we Christians are to be most pitied (1 Cor. 15:9). If Jesus Christ is the TRUTH as He says He is, then those who don't have faith in Him are lost—for eternity!

> **Jesus said to him, "I am the way, and the truth, and the**
> **life; no one comes to the Father, but through Me."**
> **John 14:6**

So, for all of us individually, whether we believe in Christ or not, we each have a terminal sin condition and are going to die one day. Have you accepted this TRUTH? Or are you in denial as to your mortality? It is not a matter of "if" you are going to die—it is a matter of "when!" That is unless Jesus Christ returns before your passing, and then it might be too late to change your mind. I mentioned in my second book that each of us is placing our bets as to whether we believe there is going to be eternal life after we die. As well, we are placing our bets as to whether there is a heaven and a hell. What do you believe? And what are you betting your eternity on? When the chips are called in and all bets are finalized, what will be the reality and truth of where you are? Have you even thought about this?

But if you on your part warn a wicked man to turn from his way, and he does not turn from his way, he will die in his iniquity; but you have delivered your life. "Now as for you, son of man, say to the house of Israel, 'Thus you have spoken, saying, "Surely our transgressions and our sins are upon us, and we are rotting away in them; how then can we survive?"' Say to them, 'As I live!' declares the Lord GOD, 'I take no pleasure in the death of the wicked, but rather that the wicked turn from his way and live. Turn back, turn back from your evil ways! Why then will you die, O house of Israel?' And you, son of man, say to your fellow citizens, 'The righteousness of a righteous man will not deliver him in the day of his transgression, and as for the wickedness of the wicked, he will not stumble because of it in the day when he turns from his wickedness; whereas a righteous man will not be able to live by his righteousness on the day when he commits sin.' When I say to the righteous he will surely live, and he *so* trusts in his righteousness that he commits iniquity, none of his righteous deeds will be remembered; but in that same iniquity of his which he has committed he will die. But when I say to the wicked, 'You will surely die,' and he turns from his sin and practices justice and righteousness, *if a* wicked man restores a pledge, pays back what he has taken by robbery, walks by the statutes which ensure life without committing iniquity, he will surely live; he shall not die. None of his sins that he has committed will be remembered against him. He has practiced justice and righteousness; he will surely live. Yet your fellow citizens say, 'The way of the Lord is not right,' when it is their own way that is not right. When the righteous turns from his righteousness and commits iniquity, then he shall die in it. But when the wicked turns from his wickedness and practices justice and righteousness, he will live by them. Yet you say, 'The way of the Lord is not right.' O house of Israel, I will judge each of you according to his ways."

Ezek. 33:9–20

May the Lord please help us if we say that we want His judgment on our lives based on how we have lived them! Sandy's reply to my question on why she would be in heaven is the most common answer I get. She is misled, as are all those who believe they are good enough to deserve heaven. Satan has them right where he wants them!

One gentleman that I asked this question gave me a not-so-common answer. When asked why he would be in heaven, he replied, "Well, Mark, I would say I would be there because I don't deserve to be in hell."

Wow! I must say that this answer is one that stopped me in my tracks! Now *that* is arrogance—wouldn't you agree? These lies to ourselves are, for the most part, just statements that the world tells us, which we repeat to ourselves and haven't really thought through carefully. The deception of the world around us is so very pervasive that we don't even reflect on what we are saying to ourselves, saying to others, or saying to God our Savior.

For those who are according to the flesh set their minds on the things of the flesh, but those who are according to the Spirit, the things of the Spirit. For the mind set on the flesh is death, but the mind set on the Spirit is life and peace, because the mind set on the flesh is hostile toward God; for it does not subject itself to the law of God, for it is not even able *to do so*; and those who are in the flesh cannot please God. However, you are not in the flesh but in the Spirit, if indeed the Spirit of God dwells in you. But if anyone does not have the Spirit of Christ, he does not belong to Him. If Christ is in you, though the body is dead because of sin, yet the spirit is alive because of righteousness. But if the Spirit of Him who raised Jesus from the dead dwells in you, He who raised Christ Jesus from the dead will also give life to your mortal bodies through His Spirit who dwells in you. So then, brethren, we are under obligation, not to the flesh, to live according to the flesh—for if you are living according to the flesh, you must die; but if by the Spirit you are putting to death the deeds of the body, you will live. For all who are being led by the Spirit of God, these are sons of God.

Rom. 8:5–14

A patient asked me one day, "Mark, what do you think the real disconnect is for people's lack of relationship with Jesus Christ?" The above Scripture speaks volumes about this. God reveals Himself to us through His Word, His Son Jesus Christ, His Holy Spirit, through His creation, those around us, and throughout our own lives as well. He allows us to have responsibility in choosing whether to respond to Him or not, and usually the main culprit in our rejecting God is our very own PRIDE. The prideful disconnect for many is that we have our minds set on the flesh—the world around us. Our minds and our lives are set on the things of this earth. We don't have a vision of where or what is in store for us from an eternal perspective because we are so wrapped up in the present. Our relationship with the world comes automatically, while a relationship with Jesus takes effort on our part. The Holy Spirit of God does not impose Himself on our lives and in our thoughts forcefully after we have received Jesus Christ as our Savior. Nor does He stand off and hold back His love and desire to infuse Himself more and more into our lives and consciousness either. Yes, He does seal us in Christ for eternity when we receive Christ as Ephesians 1:13 states. However, we each have a part in mending the disconnect that our sins helped establish and propagate.

My finding is that even though I said I was a Christian in my formative years, I really don't think I had truly received Jesus as my Lord and Savior until I was 28 years old. I claimed to know Jesus, but spent no time in relationship with Him and absolutely didn't spend *any* time in prayer and in His Word. Basically, I think I was a lost soul who had been duped and deceived by Satan into thinking I was a Christian. I was lying to myself. I didn't really discover this until I read the last book of the Bible—Revelation. I read it on a dare from a friend, and it "scared the hell out of me!" More than that, it helped me to learn that I truly didn't know the Savior that I said

I had been worshiping but wasn't. Reading that last book in the Bible made me realize that I needed to start spending time in His Word and instruction book if I truly wanted to live my life for Christ, who gave this life to me in the first place! I said I knew Christ, but I had no relationship with Him. So, in reality I didn't even know the Lord whom I said I worshiped!

If you do well, will not *your countenance* be lifted up? And if you do not do well, sin is crouching at the door; and its desire is for you, but you must master it.

Gen. 4:7

Dear friend, may I ask you another question about another "If" of our lives? All of this wrath and judgment of God on the people of the earth only pertains to those who have sinned, right? So here is the question, "Are you a sinner?" I know this is an uncomfortable question to answer but it has to have an answer, and that answer must be truthful.

"If" you are a sinner is one thing that is hard for some people to understand or contemplate. I've heard from numerous sources that one of the toughest tasks for us believers to help those nonbelievers around us to ascertain and accept, is the reality that they themselves are sinners! Satan, that scoundrel and father of lies, has pulled the wool over many eyes of those who inhabit the earth. He helps them to buy into the lie that they say to themselves: "Hey, I'm not a sinner! I'm a good person who does the right thing as best I can! I didn't ask for this sin that you say is in me, and besides, I'm better than most people out there!"

I must help you to fathom that each and every one of us is born into sin. Every person who has ever inhabited the earth

from the beginning of time is a sinner, save One—Jesus Christ!
Listen to what the Lord tells us through Paul in the book of
Romans:

> **What then? Are we better than they? Not at all; for we
> have already charged that both Jews and Greeks are all
> under sin; as it is written,**
>
> **"There is none righteous, not even one; There is none
> who understands, there is none who seeks for God; All
> have turned aside, together they have become useless;
> There is none who does good, there is not even one."**
>
> **"Their throat is an open grave, with their tongues they
> keep deceiving,"**
>
> **"The poison of asps is under their lips";**
>
> **"Whose mouth is full of cursing and bitterness";**
>
> **"Their feet are swift to shed blood, Destruction and
> misery are in their paths, And the path of peace they
> have not known."**
>
> **"There is no fear of God before their eyes."**
>
> **Rom. 3:9–18**

Hmmm. "There is no fear of God before their eyes." This
Scripture is scathing and sounds an alarm very clearly to all of
us. It warns us that each one of us is a sinner who has no claim
on being good enough to be admitted to heaven. However,
Satan would like us to be deceived into this lie to ourselves and
he is very effective with its hold on many. There is no fear of
God before their eyes because these people don't really stop
long enough in their busy schedules and quests to truly take
stock and examine themselves. "Life's too short, man!"

Do you know what? Life is short! All the more reason to

assess ourselves and make our choice as to who or what is truly important in this life, because after this life—the die has been cast, and we are in one of two places for eternity! John speaks of this deception in his first letter also:

> These things we write, so that our joy may be made complete. This is the message we have heard from Him and announce to you, that God is Light, and in Him there is no darkness at all. If we say that we have fellowship with Him and *yet* walk in the darkness, we lie and do not practice the truth; but if we walk in the Light as He Himself is in the Light, we have fellowship with one another, and the blood of Jesus His Son cleanses us from all sin. If we say that we have no sin, we are deceiving ourselves, and the truth is not in us. If we confess our sins, He is faithful and righteous to forgive us our sins and to cleanse us from all unrighteousness. If we say that we have not sinned, we make Him a liar, and His word is not in us.
>
> 1 John 1:4–10

Paul reiterates and speaks to us of our sin and our inability to earn our way to heaven in his letter to the Ephesians:

> And you were dead in your trespasses and sins, in which you formerly walked according to the course of this world, according to the prince of the power of the air, of the spirit that is now working in the sons of disobedience. Among them we too all formerly lived in the lusts of our flesh, indulging the desires of the flesh and of the mind, and were by nature children of wrath, even as the rest. But God, being rich in mercy, because of His great love with which He loved us,

even when we were dead in our transgressions, made
us alive together with Christ (by grace you have been
saved), and raised us up with Him, and seated us with
Him in the heavenly *places* in Christ Jesus, so that in
the ages to come He might show the surpassing riches
of His grace in kindness toward us in Christ Jesus. For
by grace you have been saved through faith; and that
not of yourselves, *it is* the gift of God; not as a result
of works, that no one should boast. For we are His
workmanship, created in Christ Jesus for good works,
which God prepared beforehand, that we should walk
in them.

Eph. 2:1–10

Therefore, none of us can boast that we are "good enough" to
be in heaven! If that were the case, we wouldn't need Jesus Christ
and His sacrifice for our sins. We would be our own gods, in
that our own efforts paved our way to heaven. We would be able
to shake our fists at God the Father and demand that He admit
us to be by His side in heaven, bringing with us all the filthiness
of our sins, along with our deceitful and sick hearts (Jer. 17:9).
This is the truth and reality that we find when we truly examine
ourselves and realize our sinful state.

Besides being in prayer and daily Bible study for the past 34
years, the Lord has had me on an insatiable frenzy of reading
books that have been written by giants in the faith. Some of the
more impactful authors that I've read are A.W. Tozer, Charles
Haddon Spurgeon, Andrew Murray, C.S. Lewis, Oswald
Chambers, and John MacArthur. Of late, I had a friend, Dr. Joe
McCollum, who is a close brother in Christ, introduce me to
a Welsh pastor who preached in London in the early to mid-
twentieth century. This giant in the faith has taken my walk
of faith in Christ to another level altogether over the last few

months. Not that it was at that high of a level to begin with, mind you!

His name is Martyn Lloyd-Jones and he speaks about the Beatitudes in his book *Studies in the Sermon on the Mount*,[2] as they relate to the progression of our individual walks of faith. In some of the chapters of this book, I would like to focus on these Beatitudes from a viewpoint that Lloyd-Jones exposits in his sermons in this excellent book. And no, I am no Martyn Lloyd-Jones, but I do think his main points in relating these aspects of Jesus's description of our walks with Him have opened my eyes to another perspective and insight into the amazing perfection of our Savior! So, let's take a look at the first of these timeless truths that our Lord espoused in His masterful sermon right here.

The First Beatitude

Blessed are the poor in spirit, for theirs is the kingdom of heaven.

Matt. 5:3

Many of us do not realize just how depraved and sinful we really are; in fact, we are like Sandy—we think we are good people! Until we get to the end of ourselves and realize our own unrighteousness, we have way too much confidence in ourselves and our ability. It is conducive to our sinful nature to do so. It is where I was before I was finally exposed to my dark and sinful self at that Christian concert when I was 28 years old. Before that, I felt I was doing an okay job with my walk of faith, when in reality, I was full of myself, and Jesus Christ was nowhere to be found in my life. I was not "poor in spirit"—I was full of MYSELF!

Being "poor in spirit" is not something that comes easily to most all of us. It is hard for us to really examine and look at ourselves in a truthful way because of our adeptness at lying to ourselves. We see ourselves and hold ourselves in way too high esteem. This is what the world trains us up in, and we must remember that for the present time, God is giving Satan more power over this world than he deserves—way more power! That is why the "father of lies" seems to be winning this battle on the earth at this time.

Our depravity and broken state doesn't cross our minds unless the Holy Spirit tugs at our hearts to open our eyes to our fallen state. As Martyn Lloyd-Jones says about the Beatitudes:

> Our Lord does not place them in their respective positions haphazardly or accidentally; there is what we may describe as a spiritual logical sequence to be found here. This, of necessity, is the one which must come at the beginning for good reason that there is no entry into the kingdom of heaven, or the kingdom of God, apart from it. There is no-one in the kingdom of God who is not poor in spirit. It is the fundamental characteristic of the Christian and of the citizen of the kingdom of heaven, and all the other characteristics are in a sense the result of this one.[3]

Lloyd-Jones goes on to say:

> As we go on to expound on it; we shall see that it really means an emptying, while the others are a manifestation of a fullness. We cannot be filled until we are first empty . . . It is an essential part of the gospel that conviction must always precede conversion; the gospel of Christ condemns before it releases.[4]

Let's go back to my encounter with Sandy. She thought she was going to be in heaven because she was a good person. By her answer to the question, she may not have realized her total depravity and lost state. She might be deceived and need the Lord just as much as she ever did, but she feels she is set and good to go when in reality, she isn't.

But do you know what I did? I dropped the ball! I may have planted a seed, but I didn't clarify and share the gospel message of Jesus Christ with her. I hope I see her again and get another chance. Sandy is right where I was at one time. I thought I was a believer, but now, I don't believe that I had truly received Jesus as my Savior. "If" I only get another chance!

The fear of the LORD is the beginning of knowledge; Fools despise wisdom and instruction.

Prov. 1:7

There is a way *which seems* right to a man, but its end is the way of death.

Prov. 16:25

We have considered two "Ifs" in this chapter: the "if" that we are each going to die and the "if" that each one of us is a sinner. The answer to both is yes! Are you "poor in spirit?" Or are you "full of self?" Your answer is more evident than you can even realize to those around you every day!

CHAPTER 2

YOU

There is none who understands, there is none who seeks for God; all have turned aside, together they have become useless; there is none who does good, there is not even one.

Rom. 3:11–12

The *you* that I seek to describe in this chapter is the fallen, sinful *you* that we are all born into. The fall of mankind is evident and made manifest throughout the history of our world's existence. From the first bite of the fruit in the active rebellion against God's directive by Adam and Eve, we see sin and corruption brought into this earth, and the results have been overwhelming to say the least.

That Scripture above from Romans also appeared in the first chapter and is important for us to grasp. In fact, there are other places in God's Word where our sinful nature is emphasized. One of them is here:

The fool has said in his heart, "There is no God." They are corrupt, they have committed abominable deeds; There is no one who does good. The LORD has

**looked down from heaven upon the sons of men, to
see if there are any who understand, who seek after
God. They have all turned aside; together they have
become corrupt; there is no one who does good, not
even one.**

Ps. 14:1–3

How Prideful We Are . . .

His name was David, and I had only met him a couple of times.
He was a friend and business associate of a good friend and
brother in Christ. David had called to invite me to lunch to talk
about his business. During our conversation, I was able to ask
the question: "So, David, do you mind if I ask you a personal
question?"

"Not at all," was his immediate response.

"David, I've asked this question of many different people,
and I appreciate you letting me ask it of you. If you die today,
where will you be tomorrow?"

He kind of got that deer-in-the-headlights look on his face
and stammered, "Well, I suppose I would be in heaven."

"That's great!" I said and pressed the follow-up: "Could you
tell me why you'd be there?"

That is when he gave me the unique reply I shared earlier:
"Well . . . I think because I don't deserve to be in hell."

I had to ponder and think about this response because
it caught me off guard a little. "I can understand you having
that viewpoint," I said. "My guess is that you feel you've done
nothing that warrants you being in hell, is that right?"

"Yes, I guess that would be a pretty accurate description of
how I feel."

I will discuss more about this encounter later.

Who Is the Bible Written To?

Guess how many times the word *you,* appears in the New American Standard Bible? Granted, the total number of occurrences includes the times it is used to speak of the great I AM, but it is used in the context of speaking to us mainly. The word *you* appears around 12,923 times in 7,348 verses. Now, how many times do you think the word *God* appears in that same version of the Bible? Of course, some of the times it is used with the little *g* context in *god,* but all in all, it appears about 4,355 times in 3,815 verses. So, what do you think about when you read these numbers?[5]

Does this not give us some inkling that the Bible is written primarily for us sinners, with whom the God of the universe wants to have a relationship? As I said in the first chapter, God reveals Himself to us in many and various ways. The one way that we are so adamantly averse to doing this is— wait for it—the spending of part of our time in "hungering and thirsting for righteousness" in His Word and prayer to Him. God wants a relationship with us, but we aren't willing to reciprocate and give up any of our precious time for the One Who created us! Hey, I get it! I know we are all busy with keeping up with the lives and families we have been entrusted with, but c'mon here: do you and I realize that THE GOD OF THE UNIVERSE wants us to have a relationship with Him? We are those small "y" you's . . . and we are in need of the Savior and Lord, Jesus Christ. Unfortunately, we are more apt to be like those who were responsible for the first appearance of the little "g" god in the Bible because we have our own selfish ideas.

Now when the people saw that Moses delayed to come down from the mountain, the people assembled about

Aaron, and said to him, "Come, make us a god who will go before us; as for this Moses, the man who brought us up from the land of Egypt, we do not know what has become of him.

Exod. 32:1

Remember David, who said he would be in heaven because "he didn't deserve hell?" He is deceived, as are most in this world. Again, one of the hardest tasks we believers have in discussing our faith in Christ with nonbelievers is in helping them to realize that they are sinners, lost in their sins. Yes, we believers are still sinners as well, but we have been redeemed and justified by the death of Jesus Christ Who paid the price for our sins and removed them from us as far as the east is from the west. Those who have not received Jesus as their Savior still carry their sins, and their accountability for those sins, with them—and have no relief from the consequences of those sins. They, through their pride in their own lives, have not even realized the sins they are committing day in and day out. If this gentleman believes he doesn't deserve to be in hell, then he obviously believes that his good works outweigh the bad ones. Unfortunately, more good than bad is not the standard that God uses for those He will admit into heaven for eternity. God's standard, as mentioned before, is perfect and holy righteousness—and more good than bad does not measure up to that standard.

I think if this gentleman realized what he was claiming and seriously examined his life, he would not have made the statement. Again, our failure to look at ourselves in a true and honest way is what gets us in trouble. And the world around us is sure not going to be truthful with us.

God gave Adam and Eve a shot at living the perfect and sinless life with Him in the garden, but when the choice was given as to Who or who to serve, they chose wrong. And that wrong choice has been handed down to us with our sinful nature that we are born into. Do you agree with this?

Then the LORD God took the man and put him into the garden of Eden to cultivate it and keep it. The LORD God commanded the man, saying, "From any tree of the garden you may eat freely; but from the tree of the knowledge of good and evil you shall not eat, for in the day that you eat from it you shall surely die."

Gen. 2:15–17

Guess what? Adam and Eve did eat from that tree, and they didn't die—at least physically, right there on the spot. What they did find out when they ate that fruit was that they had disobeyed God and through that disobedience, they had sinned and died spiritually. That was why they recognized they were naked and covered themselves up with whatever they could think of to hide themselves. They knew they had gone against their Creator and that they had lost the intimate fellowship they once had with Him. Once that happened, there was no way they could, on their own, retrieve that intimate fellowship and relationship with God. This loss of relationship has been passed down to all of us as well.

It is the sinful nature that is part of the warp and woof of our fallen state that keeps us in its powerful grip. We are blinded by the many distractions the world throws at us, and our minds can become numb with all the adverse stimulus that comes at us around the clock. Little by little, we get sucked in by the pervasive and overbearing world with its shameful, degrading, and corrupting influences. Pretty soon we get to a place that we do not even realize we are in our depraved state, partly because we see so much that is bad and corrupt around our world. I have told many that it is as if we are living out Romans 1. Listen to how it ends and see if you agree:

And just as they did not see fit to acknowledge God any longer, God gave them over to a depraved mind, to do those things which are not proper, being filled with all unrighteousness, wickedness, greed, evil; full of envy, murder, strife, deceit, malice; *they are* **gossips, slanderers, haters of God, insolent, arrogant, boastful, inventors of evil, disobedient to parents, without understanding, untrustworthy, unloving, unmerciful; and, although they know the ordinance of God, that those who practice such things are worthy of death, they not only do the same, but also give hearty approval to those who practice them.**

Rom. 1:28–32

Would you agree that our present culture seemingly has no shame? No one in this world wants to hide anything? In fact, the world we live in is proud of all the shameful things that are done! And to top that, the more shameful and outlandish the behavior, the better! We sinners want the world to be centered on ourselves. We want all the "likes" we can muster on our Facebook pages—whether personal or for our businesses. I mean, that's what this life is all about, right?

Social media has permeated all our mindsets as well as stolen increasing amounts of our time. It really surprised me when I was in Israel, three years ago, that these smartphones had penetrated to occupy almost all of those I walked past in and around the streets of Jerusalem. No one was looking up and out! Almost all were peering in the palm of their hands! Go out to dinner sometime and look at the tables around you at the restaurant. Chances are you will see table after table with cell phones in full glow on the faces of all or most of those seated at the table. Even when families are dining out.

With our smartphones, we each can select and choose the type of world we want to occupy and live in, our own little private kingdoms made up of the choices we each dream about and obsess over. While being so focused on our wants, we have little time to consider the wants or needs of those around us. We have no inkling of the magnet that Satan is using to draw us in and hold us in his lies and clutches. When someone wants to try to help us by pointing out our obsession, we dismiss them. Virtually none of us want to think about seriously examining ourselves and discovering what has hold of our minds and motives. Personal reflection and introspection are not our strong suit, but satisfying our many lusts and desires for the temporal is!

Why do You stand afar off, O Lord? Why do You hide Yourself in times of trouble? In pride the wicked hotly pursue the afflicted; Let them be caught in the plots which they have devised. For the wicked boasts of his heart's desire, and the greedy man curses and spurns the Lord. The wicked, in the haughtiness of his countenance, does not seek Him. All his thoughts are, "There is no God."

Ps. 10:1–4

Not only does God not hide Himself from us, He actually seeks us and stands at the door of our hearts knocking. He wants us to open our hearts and let Him in! The more we ignore Him, the more callous and leathery our hearts become—dull to the love He has shown us through His Son. In essence, we are living to ourselves and dying to our Savior, and we don't even realize it! Yes, we may have received Christ as our Lord and Savior at one time previously in our life, but over time, our commitment and resolve to stay in relationship with Him got crowded out with all the other stuff that goes on in our lives. And then we wake up one day and are jolted with a revelation: "Wow! I've grown so distant from my Savior Who loves me! How could I have been so misled as to get this far off the path from walking with Him? Look at what a mess my life and my family are in— all as a result of seeking happiness in all the wrong places and not looking for Jesus's will for my life."

> **Do not love the world nor the things in the world. If anyone loves the world, the love of the Father is not in him. For all that is in the world, the lust of the flesh and the lust of the eyes and the boastful pride of life, is not from the Father, but is from the world. And the world is passing away, and *also* its lusts; but the one who does the will of God lives forever.**
>
> **1 John 2:15–17**

The Second Beatitude

> **Blessed are those who mourn, for they shall be comforted.**
>
> **Matt. 5:4**

I used to think this was the Lord's way of comforting those who had lost a loved one. But when I read Martyn Lloyd-Jones's take on our Lord's Beatitudes, he helped me realize that acknowledging our sinful depravity makes us poor in spirit, and we then mourn our sin of pride for having believed we were good in the first place. We then have our eyes opened to what a dangerous and deceptive place Satan had brought us to and start to discover the lies we told ourselves about what our lives and actions were truly revealing. Lloyd-Jones states:

> As we saw that poverty of spirit was not something financial, but something essentially spiritual, so this again is something entirely spiritual and has nothing to do with our natural life in this world. All these Beatitudes have reference to a spiritual condition and a spiritual attitude. Those who are commended are those who mourn in spirit; they, says our Lord, are the happy people.[6]

In speaking to the high percentage of Christians who are more superficial and have a very inadequate kind of Christian life, Lloyd-Jones goes on to say:

> That is why it is so important that we should approach it all in terms of this Sermon on the Mount, which starts with negatives. We have to be poor in spirit before we can be filled with the Holy Spirit. Negative, before positive. And here again is another example of exactly the same thing—conviction must of necessity precede conversion, a real sense of sin must come before there can be a true joy of salvation. Now that is the whole essence of the gospel. So many people spend all their lives in trying to find this Christian joy. They say they would give the whole world if they could only find it, or could be like some other person who has it. Well, I suggest that in ninety-nine cases out of a hundred this is the explanation. They have failed to see that they must be convicted of sin before they can ever experience joy. They do not like the doctrine of sin. They dislike it intensely and they object to its

being preached. They want joy apart from the conviction of sin. But that is impossible; it can never be obtained. Those who are going to be converted and who wish to be truly happy and blessed are those who first of all mourn. Conviction is an essential preliminary to true conversion.[7]

Being poor in spirit and realizing our sinful state drives us to the foot of the cross, mourning and repenting of our previous self-assuredness that we pompously exemplified. Our heart is revealed to us as what it really is: **"The heart is more deceitful than all else and is desperately sick; who can understand it?" (Jer. 17:9)**

How can we get our desperately sick hearts back on track? We must repent of our sins, take a more honest and serious look at who we really are, ask for forgiveness from the only One who can give it, and then hunger and thirst for His righteousness! We must seek to do the will of the One who truly loves us! We must seek the One who will never leave our side—ever! After all, Jesus Christ came into this world to save all of us who would ever believe in Him from the sin that we each are born into. This is the gospel—the redemption and reconciling of sinful man into the perfectly righteous and holy state that each of us must have, to be able to be brought back in close relationship with the perfectly righteous and holy God of the universe! THIS IS THE STANDARD! It is God's perfect standard that is the requisite of all who will ever be in heaven. Do you and I really think we have a chance of ever living out and achieving this perfect righteousness on our own? There is no way any of us could ever achieve this, my friend! Jesus Christ is the only one Who bridges the gap of our utter depravity to enable us to be brought into His perfect and holy righteousness. A couple of the best places where this gospel is explained in the Bible are in John and Romans where God tells us very clearly:

> **No one has ascended into heaven, but He who descended from heaven: the Son of Man. As Moses lifted up the serpent in the wilderness, even so must the Son of Man be lifted up; so that whoever believes will in Him have eternal life. For God so loved the world, that He gave His only begotten Son, that whoever believes in Him shall not perish, but have eternal life. For God did not send the Son into the world to judge the world, but that the world might be saved through Him. He who believes in Him is not judged; he who does not believe has been judged already, because he has not believed in the name of the only begotten Son of God. This is the judgment, that the Light has come into the world, and men loved the darkness rather than the Light, for their deeds were evil. For everyone who does evil hates the Light, and does not come to the Light for fear that his deeds will be exposed. But he who practices the truth comes to the Light, so that his deeds may be manifested as having been wrought in God.**
>
> **John 3:13–21**

And here in Romans 3, God explains more in depth how Jesus's death on the cross atoned for our sins. Some refer to this as the "heart" of the gospel:

> **Now we know that whatever the Law says, it speaks to those who are under the Law, that every mouth may be closed, and all the world may become accountable**

to God; because by the works of the Law no flesh will be justified in His sight; for through the Law *comes* the knowledge of sin. But now apart from the Law *the* righteousness of God has been manifested, being witnessed by the Law and the Prophets, even *the* righteousness of God through faith in Jesus Christ for all those who believe; for there is no distinction; for all have sinned and fall short of the glory of God, being justified as a gift by His grace through the redemption which is in Christ Jesus; whom God displayed publicly as a propitiation in His blood through faith. *This was* to demonstrate His righteousness, because in the forbearance of God He passed over the sins previously committed; for the demonstration, *I say*, of His righteousness at the present time, so that He might be just and the justifier of the one who has faith in Jesus. Where then is boasting? It is excluded. By what kind of law? Of works? No, but by a law of faith. For we maintain that a man is justified by faith apart from works of the Law. Or is God *the God* of Jews only? Is He not *the God* of Gentiles also? Yes, of Gentiles also, since indeed God who will justify the circumcised by faith and the uncircumcised through faith is one. Do we then nullify the Law through faith? May it never be! On the contrary, we establish the Law.

Rom. 3:19–31

These verses speak to God's solution for redeeming and reconciling sinful man back to Himself for eternity. But, as sinful men and women, we must receive and listen to what our Lord says to us in regard to this plan. If our plan is all we want to consider, so be it—God will allow us to do that and remain apart from Him—forever if we want. It is our individual choice as to what we will avail ourselves to.

God's Word was written down by men who were carried by God's Holy Spirit to do so. The more time one spends in this Holy Word, the more convinced of this fact he becomes. I myself can attest to this. Before I received Jesus as my Lord, I was right where you may find yourself right now. I thought I was that "good person" who was going to heaven by my own good deeds. I hadn't read virtually anything in the Bible—I felt I didn't need to do so. So, when I started reading it, all of these words and phrases were like trying to read a foreign language. But the Lord gave me, just as He will give you, more and more understanding of what He is saying to you through this Word, as you spend time in it. Remember Hebrews 4:12, in the Preface, that said that God's Word is "living and active?" It is!

Availing ourselves to God's Word on a daily basis will impact and change us to help us begin "thinking" in a right manner—both about God . . . and about ourselves. Are you happy with the way your life is going and the *you* that you have become? Is your family at a place where you feel "all is good, we don't need any help?" If it is, then congratulations! You're the first person I've run across that feels that way.

Are you mourning your own sin? Or are you still in denial that you even sin at all? You'll hear it again, "Let's take a videotape of all your thoughts and actions over the last 24 hours and play it for all to see and listen to . . . !"

Are there any takers? I thought not. We cannot be comforted and redeemed if we feel we have no need of either. Pride is such a terrible thing, and it will lead to the death of many! Will you be one of them? Don't kid yourself—as sinners, we all deserve hell. Jesus Christ and His sacrificial death and atonement on the cross is the only way the gap between sin and righteousness can be bridged.

So, where are *you*? Which *you* is in control of your life? The dying and prideful you? Or the humble, mourning, and servant you? And please don't try to ignore these questions, because deep down, you know that they are relevant to you—and are meaningful questions that deserve an answer!

CHAPTER 3

DIE

**Therefore I said to you, that you will die in your sins;
for unless you believe that I am *He*, you will die in
your sins.**

John 8:24

Death is a difficult subject for most of us to talk about. We
like to tuck the thought of it back into the far recesses of
our minds, so we don't have to really ponder that it is an ever-
present reality for us.

Guess who was speaking here in the verse above? Jesus
Christ was making Himself perfectly clear, as He did so much
of the time. A lot of the problem with His message was that
people didn't want to hear it. The Pharisees were experts at nit-
picking and ascribing rules to the *letter* of the law. They were
miserable failures at understanding the *spirit* of the law. This
is shown by the many rules and traditions that they added to
Moses's original law which God had given. We have similar
obstacles in our beliefs and have a difficult time ascribing a
definition of *truth* in our culture and society today. That is why
verses in the Bible, like the one above, raise the hair on many

people's necks as they read them. Here is another one that rubs many the wrong way, I spoke of it in the Preface:

For the word of God is living and active and sharper than any two-edged sword, and piercing as far as the division of soul and spirit, of both joints and marrow, and able to judge the thoughts and intentions of the heart. And there is no creature hidden from His sight, but all things are open and laid bare to the eyes of Him with whom we have to do.

Heb. 4:12–13

God is sharing that His Word, the Bible, is His living and active means of sharing Himself with those who seek Him. There is nothing else on this earth that compares with the Bible. For thousands of years, people have tried to discount it, make fun of it, and disprove its validity and truthfulness. The prophecies of Christ and historical facts make the Bible the most amazing document on the entire planet. While espousing the truth of God almighty, the Bible likewise speaks to our brokenness and depravity. Given all that, we don't like having our thoughts and intentions judged. After all, they are ours, aren't they? Face it, we don't like to look truthfully at why we do the things we do. We just want to do them and not think about why.

I was teaching an adult Sunday School class that Joseph, my son, came to when he was home from college one weekend. We were discussing our lack of willingness, as Christians, to spend time in prayer and in our Bibles. I asked the class why this was so. Everyone said busyness was the main issue, but I posed another explanation: "I think most of us don't like spending time in the Scriptures because when we read and study them, they bring us to a keener realization and exposure of our sins. And we don't like to have our sins brought before us daily. If we can just get by with hearing about them one day of the week, on Sunday, that is easier to deal with, because we can move on down the road we each want to pursue without being reminded that we are getting off track."

Join these two previous references together along with others and you eventually get to a conclusion. Either Jesus was speaking the truth when He made the claims in that first verse (John 8:24), or He was lying—it can be only one of the two. That is a very strong and unambiguous claim to make to people in general. He proclaims the same clarity and resultant outcome in numerous other places in the Bible, stating that He is one with God the Father and that there is no other way but through Him to be saved from our sinful state. With that in mind, how do we engage those we come in contact with each day?

Do We Engage in Meaningful and Impactful Conversations?

I was having breakfast with my friend Charles, whom I've known for the past 33 years through business. He and I have never been best friends, but we knew one another well enough for him to share that he had lost his Dad to a heart attack when he was in his teens. We had discussed how difficult that had been for him. That loss had possibly skewed his opinion about whether there is a loving God because, "How could a loving God let his Dad die at such a young age and take him from this son who loved him so much?"

Charles always referred to himself as an atheist. He knew, however, that I was a Christian almost from the start, even though I wasn't very strong in my faith in those early years of our friendship. We don't see each other often, maybe two or three times a year, and I had given him a copy of both of my books when they came out.

At a breakfast meeting one morning, he said, "You know, Mark, I've not been looking forward to this breakfast because I knew I hadn't read any of your new book you gave me. This meeting gave me impetus to skim through and read about the first half of it over the last couple of days, and I have to confess, you say some things that make one think."

"Charles, don't worry about having to read the book; that won't make or break our friendship. I do appreciate you taking the time to look at it and read some of it, even if you were rushed in doing so. Has anything stuck out to you from what you have read in it?"

"Yeah it has. You know how you put those Bible verses in it, dispersed throughout your writing? I look at those and read them, and I can't make heads or tails out of them. And you know, men wrote that Bible and they are prone to make mistakes."

With those comments Charles made in mind, I ask you to read the following from God's Holy Word:

For to us God revealed *them* through the Spirit; for the Spirit searches all things, even the depths of God. For who among men knows the *thoughts* of a man except the spirit of the man, which is in him? Even so the *thoughts* of God no one knows except the Spirit of God. Now we have received, not the spirit of the world, but the Spirit who is from God, that we might know the things freely given to us by God, which things we also speak, not in words taught by human wisdom, but in those taught by the Spirit, combining spiritual *thoughts* with spiritual *words*. But a natural man does not accept

**the things of the Spirit of God; for they are foolishness
to him, and he cannot understand them, because they
are spiritually appraised.**

1 Cor. 2:10–14

My response to his comment was this: "I can understand
that, Charles. I felt the same way when I started reading the
Bible. It does get more understandable if you stay with it
though."

"Well, you and I know that's not going to happen!" he joked.

"Charles, do you mind if I ask you a question?

"Sure, what's up?"

"Do you believe there is a heaven?"

"Well, yes, I believe there is an afterlife of some sort. You
know, we use so little of our brain capacity. I think that when
we die, it will be as if our brain explodes into oneness with the
Cosmos of ultimate consciousness."

So, I asked the next question, "So, do you believe that there
is a hell?"

"Oh no, absolutely not. There is no hell!"

"No Satan or devil then?"

"No, I don't believe there is a little man running around
in a red suit with a pointy tail and a pitchfork." He said this
somewhat laughingly.

"Charles, do you mind if I ask you another question that
I've asked a lot of people, especially those who tell me that they
don't believe there is a God?"

"Sure!"

"If you die today, where will you be tomorrow?"

"I'd be in the grave, six-feet under!"

"So, what about that oneness with the Cosmos you spoke
of?"

"Well, I think our minds will have their consciousness, but our bodies will be dead and gone."

"What if you're mistaken?"

"I guess I'll be wherever that leads me then."

(One year later: a follow-up on Charles . . .)

One to two weeks before I was finishing the manuscript on this book, Charles and I met again, and I told him the third book was almost done. He said, "Great, so what's the title to this one?"

I shared the title with him and then told him, "By the way, you're in it!"

"No way!"

"Yup! You wanna read that part right quick and see if I made any mistakes?"

"Sure, let's see it." Charles read the previous text you just got through and said, "It's pretty accurate, but you got one thing wrong. My Dad died of cancer, not a heart attack, when I was 17. It was my Mother who died of a heart attack when I was 22!"

You could have knocked me over with a feather as I grappled with what he had just shared. All these years he and I had spent in discussions, and I hadn't known that his Mother had died so early in his life as well.

"Yeah, I've been pretty much alone since I was 22, Mark."

"Charles, I had never heard that part of your story! I am so very sorry!"

"Hey, it is what it is. What else can I say?"

We finished our visit, and I walked him out to his car. Again, I let him know how sorry I was for the early loss of both of his parents.

We were standing by his car when I said, "Charles, I just want you to know one thing." I began tearing up. "There is not a

morning that goes by that I don't pray for Charles Jones. I pray
for you every morning and have been for the past few years. I
love you Charles! But know this: Jesus Christ loves you more
than anyone else possibly could!"

He looked at me as if a weight had been taken off his
shoulders, and the relief from that weight was bringing tears
to his eyes. He took a step toward me and hugged me in a way
that let me know he loved me too! He started sobbing, I started
sobbing, and we held onto each other. I'm still praying that the
Lord Jesus Christ will draw Charles to Himself!

Many Have No Clue Where the Paths They're Traveling Will Lead Them

> For the ways of a man are before the eyes of the LORD,
> And He watches all his paths. His own iniquities will
> capture the wicked, and he will be held with the cords
> of his sin. He will die for lack of instruction, and in the
> greatness of his folly he will go astray.
>
> **Prov. 5:21–23**

> The lips of the righteous feed many, but fools die for
> lack of understanding.
>
> **Prov. 10:21**

> There is a way *which seems* right to a man, but its end is
> the way of death.
>
> **Prov. 14:12**

Death, again, is a hard topic to broach for many of us in this
"self-centered" world. I've asked this question of many, and
there is almost always a sort of dumbfounded and quizzical

look that comes from it. Why? We avoid speaking of death because we don't want to think about the eternal ramifications of it. We don't want to consider what will come after, because we can't see it, put a label on it, and define the outcome in absolute terms. Here is another aspect of death to consider, and that is what leads to it—it is sin. Sin always leads to death! It destroys man and leads us onward in a march to the grave. That is one of the reasons why none of us likes to talk about either of these topics—sin or death! They make us think about what we are doing with our lives right now. And we don't like to examine ourselves to even consider our actions. We like to be and do what we each want to be and do. We also don't want to live our lives by any other standards than our own. After all, "It's my life!" we all say.

Do you know what? It is! It is each of our own lives! That's what makes all the results of sin and death so very important for each of us to understand. We need to understand what is at stake in these two unescapable traits we each possess. Do you know why? It is because what we do and choose in this life matters! The actions and choices we make about what we do and what we believe determine what will be the final destination for each of our eternities. And we will each live an eternity in one of two places after this life on earth is gone. And wherever we end up will be the forever that we occupy. Atheists believe there is no life of any kind after death. They think that the talk about eternity is just hot air and that there is no eternity, much less two totally different destinations. To try to simplify these two places, think of one place as full of glorious awesomeness in the presence of God Almighty— full of love, light, and joy for all that are there! And the other place is where those who choose to reject God and not believe in Jesus Christ can get what they want. They get to be apart from God at a place where God Almighty chooses not to be.

God, therefore, gives them what they want—a place of hatred, pride, total darkness, and agony apart from the God they loathed! Which of these two places would you long to be in for eternity? You might want to think about it, because each of us will be in one place or the other.

So, if sin leads to death for us all, how will we each deal with that sin? Sin has consequences and those consequences reach all the way into heaven itself, as Martyn Lloyd-Jones says in his book *Studies on the Sermon on the Mount*:

> Sin in you and in me is something that caused the Son of God to sweat drops of blood in the Garden of Gethsemane. It caused Him to endure all the agony and the suffering to which He was subjected. And finally, it caused Him to die upon the cross. That is sin. We can never remind ourselves of that too frequently. Is it not our danger—I think we all must admit—to think of sin merely in terms of ideas of morality, to catalogue sins and to divide them into great and small, and various other classifications? There is a sense, no doubt, in which there is some truth in these ideas: but there is another sense in which such classifications are all wrong and indeed dangerous. For sin is sin, and always sin; that is what our Lord is emphasizing. It is not for example, only the act of adultery; it is the thought, and the desire also which is sinful.[8]

A little later in the same chapter, Lloyd-Jones says:

> "Do we all realize that the most important thing we have to do in this world is to prepare ourselves for eternity?"[9]

Apparently not, wouldn't you agree? We don't talk about eternity very much. In reality, we virtually avoid the topic at any cost. Yet, God has set eternity in all of our hearts:

He has made everything appropriate in its time. He has also set eternity in their heart, yet so that man will not find out the work which God has done from the beginning even to the end.

Eccles. 3:11

"You are My witnesses," declares the LORD, "And My servant whom I have chosen, in order that you may know and believe Me, and understand that I am He. Before Me there was no God formed, and there will be none after Me. I, even I, am the LORD; and there is no savior besides Me. It is I who have declared and saved and proclaimed, and there was no strange *god* among you; so you are My witnesses," declares the LORD, "And I am God. Even from eternity I am He; and there is none who can deliver out of My hand; I act and who can reverse it?"

Isa. 43:10–13

But as for you, Bethlehem Ephrathah, *too* little to be among the clans of Judah, from you One will go forth for Me to be ruler in Israel. His goings forth are from long ago, from the days of eternity. Therefore, He will give them *up* until the time when she who is in labor has borne a child. Then the remainder of His brethren will return to the sons of Israel. And He will arise and shepherd *His flock* in the strength of the LORD, in the majesty of the name of the LORD His God. And they

will remain, because at that time He will be great to the ends of the earth.

Mic. 5:2-4

For this reason I remind you to kindle afresh the gift of God which is in you through the laying on of my hands. For God has not given us a spirit of timidity, but of power and love and discipline. Therefore do not be ashamed of the testimony of our Lord, or of me His prisoner; but join with *me* in suffering for the gospel according to the power of God, who has saved us, and called us with a holy calling, not according to our works, but according to His own purpose and grace which was granted us in Christ Jesus from all eternity, but now has been revealed by the appearing of our Savior Christ Jesus, who abolished death, and brought life and immortality to light through the gospel, for which I was appointed a preacher and an apostle and a teacher. For this reason I also suffer these things, but I am not ashamed; for I know whom I have believed and I am convinced that He is able to guard what I have entrusted to Him until that day. Retain the standard of sound words which you have heard from me, in the faith and love which are in Christ Jesus. Guard, through the Holy Spirit who dwells in us, the treasure which has been entrusted to *you.*

2 Tim. 1:6-14

We believers in Christ have each been entrusted with the Holy Spirit living within us who gives us spiritual life that cannot die. How are we doing at presenting ourselves as living and holy sacrifices?

Therefore I urge you, brethren, by the mercies of God, to present your bodies a living and holy sacrifice, acceptable to God, *which is* your spiritual service of worship. And do not be conformed to this world, but be transformed by the renewing of your mind, that you may prove what the will of God is, that which is good and acceptable and perfect.

Rom. 12:1–2

This is something that the Lord has placed in my heart with a passion: each of us will live forever! Why the passion? Because it is obvious that most of those people around us are living their lives as if today is the only thing that is important, that their wants are all that consume them, and that there is no need to be concerned about what will happen after they die. Therefore, many are walking right into Satan's trap of hell with their eyes wide open and being totally blinded to where they could be for eternity. This will be their destiny if they don't hear the good news of the gospel of Jesus Christ and receive Him as the only One Who can save them from that horrendous place!

One weekend, I played golf with two buddies from my dental school years. It had been about 10 to 15 years since I had visited with one of them, and I gave him both of my previous books. He texted me four days later to tell me that he had just finished reading not one, but both books in those four days. I texted him back to see if he had speed-read them so fast that he may not have gotten anything out of them. His response let me know he had read them thoroughly. His first text said, "My favorite thing is, what you say is the only thing we can take to heaven: a friend." His second was, "I just got my faith jump-started; your books woke my lazy self up!"

I had heard the comment from Larry Moyer about eight years ago when he said, "You know there is only one thing that you can take to heaven; a friend!" That one statement by that man has so impacted me and my purpose for living. It has, because it is so very true! Death is such a difficult subject for people. Why not give them hope for where they will be afterward—for eternity?

The Third Beatitude

Blessed are the gentle, for they shall inherit the earth.
                                                    Matt. 5:5

Again, the way the Lord ordered and spoke these Beatitudes guides and directs us in our walk with Him. It is astounding, and I keep asking myself, "Why didn't I see this before?" But I should know by now that this is the case with our God's Holy and Living Word! Rather than speaking to the gentle and meek, Jesus meant this Beatitude for all of us. I originally felt these words did not pertain to me, because I am not gentle and meek. While others may be nonconfrontational and gentle in spirit, that is not one of my strong suits. When I discovered this verse was for all of us, my heart changed!

Lloyd-Jones comments again:

Once more, then, we are reminded at the very beginning that the Christian is altogether different from the world. It is a difference in quality, an essential difference. He is a new man, a new creation; he belongs to an entirely different kingdom. And not only is the world unlike him; it cannot possibly understand him. He is an enigma to the world. And if you and I are not, in this primary sense, problems and enigmas to the non-Christians around us, then this tells us a great deal about our profession of the Christian faith.[10]

Lloyd-Jones goes on to say this about meekness:

What, then, is meekness? I think we can sum it up in this way. Meekness is essentially a true view of oneself, expressing itself in attitude and conduct with respect to others. It is therefore two things. It is my attitude towards myself, and it is an expression of that in my relationship to others. You see how inevitably it follows being 'poor in spirit' and 'mourning.' A man can never be meek unless he is poor in spirit. A man can never be meek unless he has seen himself as a vile sinner. These other things must come first. But when I have that true view of myself in terms of poverty of spirit, and mourning because of my sinfulness, I am led on to see that there must be an absence of pride. The meek man is not proud of himself, he does not in any sense glory in himself. He feels that there is nothing in himself of which he can boast. It also means that he does not assert himself.[11]

If we are being emptied of ourselves and are dying to ourselves, there is no longer any room for boastful pride and pushing ourselves and our views onto those around us. We have a calmer and more gracious demeanor that we exhibit because of the newfound humility that we have never had before in our lives. We take other's feelings and opinions in a more compassionate and loving way, while being less and less confrontational and combative in our responses to their views and actions.

Do you know what starts happening to us when we become poor in spirit, mourn our own sin, and develop gentleness and meekness in our lives? This is when we can see ourselves becoming less self-centered and more Christ-centered. This then leads us to become more other-centered, looking for ways to serve others' needs and not our own. In effect, we are being transformed "in Christ"—to that which God created us to be. Again, I must hand it to Dr. McCollum. He got me started reading Martyn Lloyd-Jones, and I have found him to be very insightful in his expository sharing of the Word of God. Before I started reading *Studies in the Sermon on the Mount*, I read somewhere that Lloyd-Jones's commentary on Romans 6 entitled *The New Man*,[12] was considered by many to be a pivotal study on their walks of faith. When I read something like that, I take note. Guess what? They were right!

From Martyn Lloyd-Jones's Book on Romans 6— *The New Man*—on Love . . .

As I began reading this book, it was evident to me that this man, through the Holy Spirit's prompting, had insights into the Holy Word that were going to impact me greatly.

I shared in my first book—*Which Way Is Up?*—that the Lord had helped me to understand His purpose for my life back in 1990, when I was 36 years old. That year, the Holy Spirit revealed my "purpose statement" for my life in Christ to me at a retreat I attended. What He shared stuck with me for 27 years, and I was convinced that it was not to be improved upon. Pride in self and being assured that we have a lock on our faith is a dangerous place to be. Humility and perseverance in seeking Christ should be our lone goal! I had missed something, and it is probably not the only thing I will ever miss in regard to this purpose either. As we pursue Jesus, He reveals more and more of Himself to us, so we need to stay very humble—there is NEVER any room for pride!

What did I miss? What I wrote in 1990 as my life's purpose was this: "I am here to serve the Lord Who sent me; to serve those He sends to me; with reverence and humility for His glory."[13] I used it in both of my previous books. Pretty good, huh? I was so proud of this revelation to me back then. I gloried in the profoundness and completeness that I perceived it had. (Sounds like someone was in an "I coma!")

As I read this commentary on Romans 6, I was very impacted, and at one-point, Lloyd-Jones pointed me to this Scripture in a way I had never thought about before. The verse? It was Ephesians 1:4: **"Just as He chose us in Him before the foundation of the world, that we should be holy and blameless before Him. In love."**

The last two words hooked me—*in love*! I had missed this aspect in all my pursuit of serving my God and serving those around me. As it says in 1 Corinthians 13:1–2:

If I speak with the tongues of men and of angels, but do not have love, I have become a noisy gong or a clanging cymbal. And if I have *the gift of* prophecy, and know all mysteries and all knowledge; and if I have all faith, so as to remove mountains, but do not have love, I am nothing.

I had left out the most important aspect of what Jesus Christ wanted me to do all along. Oh yes, I do think I showed love in many ways through all those 27 years, but this slapped me across the face like a cold, wet towel! And I needed it!

Now my purpose for being is changed and changed for the better, and do you know what? I'm sure it will change again, as the Lord grows me! Here is my purpose now: I am here to serve my Lord Who sent me; to serve those He sends to me; with reverence, humility, and the love of Christ; all for His glory.

THIS is now why I am here! How about you? Do you know why you are here on this earth?

Jesus is not as concerned with what we *do* as He is with what we *are*. This is His primary concern! What we *do*, is only important in relationship with what we *are*. Here it is again, and we each need to hear and consider this over and over in thinking about why we do the things we do. What is our "heart motive?" If we are not careful, Satan convinces us that *we each* are to be on the throne of our hearts, not Jesus Christ.

You see it evidenced all around. People doing things with the motivation to be noticed by the people around them. All the while, Jesus knows their true motivation within their hearts is flawed and they are carrying out their quests with hearts that are deceitful and misleading. They are concerned with—you guessed it—themselves and the notoriety and strokes they can get from others for their actions! I know this first hand because I repeatedly question myself as to what my motivation is for doing these books, texting the devotionals in the morning, passing out the Scripture references, and other efforts. One thing I can assure you, the books have not been a profit center for Keyea's and my retirement. In fact, they have been a drain! This in part helps me trust in Christ, that He wants me to do these, because I never set out to write them. Christ is the One Who motivated me to do them. After all, it is His money anyway, and I figure that if He wants me to do these, Christ will care for all my family's needs. He has never let us down through all these years.

What I am saying is that *I am now* different than *I was* before. Jesus has helped me to have different motives and different goals than I once had. And I *can* say that my life is so much more joyous now than it ever was previously! Every day has purpose now! I truly do feel that the Lord is giving me the abundant life that He promised.

As the Holy Spirit has enabled me to change in my purpose and perspective, I have found that this life is not all about me. In fact, it is not about me at all. It is all about Christ and those He sends across my path. Jesus is helping me to die to my wants and needs while looking to His wants and will for this life He has given me. Also, He is opening my eyes to the heartaches and needs of those I come in contact with each day, every day. Dying to self means just that—me decreasing and Christ increasing as John 3:30 says: **"He must increase, but I must decrease."**

Why do you do the things you do? What is your heart motive for all you do? There are only two beings that know for certain why you do the things you do—Jesus and you!

What are you living for? What will you die for? We will each die to something! Will we die to the world, to ourselves, to those around us, or are we dying to Jesus Christ?

CHAPTER 4

TODAY

I call heaven and earth to witness against you today, that I have set before you life and death, the blessing and the curse. So choose life in order that you may live, you and your descendants.

Deut. 30:19

Each day we are given on this earth is another opportunity at a new start in this life—so to speak. Is this an overstatement? I don't think so. We can start the new day with the same bleary-eyed stumbling around in the dark—shuffling around trying to hurry and get ready because yet again, we slept in too long. And we ask ourselves, "Why did I stay up so late?"

Or we can go to bed early and look forward to the morning and spending time with our Lord in prayer, in relationship, and in His Word. I have to say that my early morning time with Christ is my favorite time of the day. Jesus listens to me and I listen to Him. We commune and share our lives with one another through prayer and His Holy Word. I have found that getting up between 3:30 and 4:30 a.m. has become the routine of my life—7 days a week, 365 days a year. Jesus helps me to get ready for a day of being focused on eternity, Him, and His will.

Opportunities Abound . . . Even in Short Time Spans . . .

I don't even know his name, but I do know that he was 70 years old because he told me! We were skiing on Spring Break in Telluride with long-time friends, an event which has been one of the highlights during each of the last 15 years for our family. The annual time of getting together has created lifetime memories and friendships between two families that will stretch on into eternity, as all family members are believers in our Savior. Each year, there are opportunities that arise, which can catch us off-guard at times, as we are among many people on the slopes who have no faith in Christ or who profess faith in something—they just aren't sure what that something is.

Such was the case on a long chairlift I happened to be riding on, seated between two total strangers. I like riding on a chairlift with those I've never met, how about you? I enjoy finding out where people are from, what they do for a living, the makeup of their family, etc. Being an outgoing extrovert, I am usually the one initiating conversations among those who might remain silent for the 8- to 15-minute ride, depending on stops and starts and length of the lift. This ride was different, and I welcomed it with open arms!

The lady in her 50s on my left never said a word the entire ride, but not so for the gentleman on the right.

"So, what do you do for a living?" he asked right off the bat.

"I'm a dentist down in the Houston area."

"How about that. You know I've been blessed that I haven't had to spend a lot of time in you guy's chairs. I just get them cleaned and that's about all I've had to do all my life—I'm really blessed in that regard," he said.

That was my cue, so I took the bait. "You really are blessed. I know of a lot of people that would love to be able to make that statement. Where are you from?"

"Oh, I live about 30 minutes away toward Ridgeway."

"You know, it sounds like you might have an interest in the books I've written."

"What are the books about?" he asked.

"They are about faith—faith in Jesus Christ."

"Well, I'm a Catholic and was in parochial schools all of my youth."

"That's great! I'm working on the third book right now," I said. "In fact, you could help me. Can I ask you a personal question?"

"Sure."

I turned my head to catch his eyes opening wider as I asked, "If you die today, where will you be tomorrow?"

He laughed initially; then got more serious with a furrow in his brow as he contemplated this poignant query. "You know, I've thought about that, believe it or not! I would hope I would be in heaven."

"Would you not be sure that you would be there?"

"That's difficult to totally be sure of. You see, I think there are going to be two very long lines. One line will be full of people going to heaven, and the other would be going to the other place—you know, the bad place."

"What will determine which line you will be in?" was my next question.

"I guess whether I've been good enough to be in that line going to heaven. I just hope I'll be in the right line."

The chairlift was approaching the top of the mountain, so I said, "Remember to look up Amazon-books for a book titled *Which Way Is Up?* It will have some answers for you on how you can be assured you'll be in heaven. Just remember we can't earn it or be good enough to be in heaven—it is a gift of grace and mercy, through the atoning death of Jesus Christ and His paying the price for our sins."

With that, we were off and out of the chair. He skied off saying, "Thanks, I will! Nice meeting you. Good luck with the books!"

The lady on my left had pulled off to the side of the ski trail and had her phone out looking something up on it. I wonder!

Are We Wasting the Privilege?

But having the same spirit of faith, according to what is written, "I believed, therefore I spoke," we also believe, therefore we also speak; knowing that He who raised the Lord Jesus will raise us also with Jesus and will present us with you. For all things *are* for your sakes, that the grace which is spreading to more and more people may cause the giving of thanks to abound to the glory of God. Therefore we do not lose heart, but though our outer man is decaying, yet our inner man is being renewed day by day. For momentary, light affliction is producing for us an eternal weight of glory far beyond all comparison, while we look not at the things which are seen, but at the things which are not seen; for the things which are seen are temporal, but the things which are not seen are eternal.

2 Cor. 4:13–18

Listen, when you get to be 63 years old, as I am, you realize every day that this outer man—the body—is decaying! Have you ever given serious thought and consideration to what the gift of each day really is? How about the gift of the nighttime for rest and recovery of our weary bodies? What about the escape from the misaligned and chaotic day we may have had the day before? Or the lingering and beautiful memories of a previous day in which everything went absolutely perfect?

We each have only so many days on this earth, and with each one that passes, we are one day closer to the time when we will have no more of them left. Each day is a gift! So, what are we doing with the gift of each day? Each one is a do-over, right? An opportunity to have a closer relationship with those in our family, with those at our workplace, and with the Savior Who put us here. If we break it down, we each have little "mini-lives" to live out each day. My question to each one of us is this: "How many of these gifted days are we wasting?"

Only you and the Lord know the answer to that question! Does it bother you that He knows? It might, because numerous places in His Word let us know that we will each have to give an account of what we did with our lives on this earth. Will we have regrets for actions taken as well as opportunities ignored or lost? Absolutely we will. I watched a video of a talk Anne Graham Lotz gave in which she states something to the effect, "You know each one of us will have to face our Savior and give an account of our lives to Him. We will all have regrets, but I hope to have as few of those regrets as possible."[14]

Don't we all! I've been involved in daily Bible study for over 34 years now and still regret the time I wasted in high school, college, and my mid-twenties. I wreaked a lot of heartache for others and myself during that time. Likewise, I have had men and women state that they wish they had lived many of their previous years differently as well. You know what? We can't get them back! We cannot relive them. We can learn from them and redeem them from the ashes by turning them over to Christ and using the experiences we had in them to enable us to better relate to those around us who are living similar lives of lostness that we ourselves were. And yes, we can reconnect with those we wronged or were wronged by, in order to impact them for Christ by showing them the love of Christ.

For we must all appear before the judgment seat of Christ, that each one may be recompensed for his deeds in the body, according to what he has done, whether good or bad.

2 Cor. 5:10

But you, why do you judge your brother? Or you again, why do you regard your brother with contempt? For we will all stand before the judgment seat of God. For it is written, "As I live, says the LORD, every knee shall bow to Me, and every tongue shall give praise to God." So then each one of us will give account of himself to God.

Romans 14:10–12

I don't know about you, but these Scriptures give me pause and make me reflect on what I am doing with my life each day. It is too easy just to "muddle along" with the crowd in this world, floating down the tidal wave to the cesspool that it seems to be headed toward. Living a life for our Savior and those He sends our way requires effort, sometimes massive effort. We, as individuals, can make a difference in that spiraling down of the world around us—through our Lord Jesus Christ and His Indwelling Holy Spirit. That is, if we will avail ourselves to Him.

So, it surprised me when I had a gentleman of utmost integrity, who has lived a strong and unflinching life of faith in our Savior, make this comment in my office one day: "You know Mark, I am getting to a place in my life where I would like to have it be of significance. You know . . . be meaningful and impactful."

The reason I was so surprised was the humility involved! He didn't know! He didn't even know! I've been watching this man for the last 10 years, and I've seen nothing but significance, meaning, and impact on a hurting world from him! He didn't even know that he didn't know—how impactful for Christ he has been! Now THAT is where I want to be! You see, this man has been so wrapped up in his relationship with Christ, in serving Christ, and serving those around him with the right motives, that he has been LOST—to himself. Did you get that? He has been so loving Christ and loving those Christ has sent to him, that he has been oblivious that he has shown the love of Christ in a huge way for all of us around him to see. Now THAT is humility! That is a man being Christlike! That is living each day as if it were your last one on earth! His life has already been significant and impactful—and he doesn't even realize it!

As Oswald Chambers says in his book *My Utmost for His Highest*:

> **"These things I have spoken to you, that My joy may be in you, and *that* your joy may be made full" (John 15:11).** What was the joy that Jesus had? Joy should not be confused with happiness. In fact, it is an insult to Jesus Christ to use the word *happiness* in connection with Him. The joy of Jesus was His absolute self-surrender and self-sacrifice to His Father— the joy of doing that which the Father sent Him to do—**" . . . who for the joy that was set before Him endured the cross . . . (Heb. 12:2). I delight to do Your will, O my God . . ."(Ps. 40:8).** Jesus prayed that our joy might continue fulfilling itself until it becomes the same joy as His. Have I allowed Jesus Christ to introduce His joy to me?

Living a full and overflowing life does not rest in bodily health, in circumstances, nor even in seeing God's work succeed, but in the perfect understanding of God, and in the same fellowship and oneness with Him that Jesus Himself enjoyed. But the first thing that will hinder this joy is the subtle irritability caused by giving too much thought to our circumstances. Jesus said, " . . . **the cares of this world, . . . choke the word, and it becomes unfruitful"** (Mark 4:19). And before we even realize what has happened, we are caught up in our cares. All that God has done for us is merely the threshold—He wants us to come to the place where we will be His witnesses and proclaim who Jesus is.

Have the right relationship with God, finding your joy there, and out of you **"will flow rivers of living water"** (John 7:38). Be a fountain through which Jesus can pour His "living water." Stop being hypocritical and proud, aware only of yourself, and live **"your life . . . hidden with Christ in God"** (Col. 3:3). A person who has the right relationship with God lives a life as natural as breathing wherever he goes. The lives that have been the greatest blessing to you are the lives of those people who themselves were unaware of having been a blessing.[15]

The Fourth Beatitude

Blessed are those who hunger and thirst for righteousness, for they shall be satisfied.

Matt. 5:6

As I have said elsewhere numerous times, this *hungering and thirsting for righteousness* is THE PLACE of our most common *disconnect* with our Lord. We are a busy people, in a busy and misled world that many say seems to be cascading down a spiraling path to destruction. Many are aghast at the rapidity and the degree of breakdown of the family unit that is rampant in the world we are living in! The only way we are going to be able to do anything to reverse this trend is to avail ourselves to a more vibrant and meaningful relationship with our Savior.

I hear this comment all the time from those I urge to spend time each morning with our Lord, "Mark, I know I should, but I just can't find the time to spend in prayer and Bible study each day with Jesus—I'm so busy!"

What we don't understand is that our "busyness" is actually keeping us from the most important relationship we can seek to have on this earth. After listening to this excuse from so many for years and years now, the Lord put it on my heart a couple of years back to start sending out a devotional text each morning to people around me to try to help them begin spending daily time with our Lord. Here is the explanation I send out when I'm introducing someone to the texts. An actual morning text follows:

Devotional texts explanation . . .

Ingrid,

I have been sending out a morning devotional text to what started at 100 and is now over 300 people (including eight pastors) each morning for about two years now. I haven't missed a day yet—other than a 4-day stint that arose from a technical glitch . . .

It is an effort the Lord put on my heart to help those who

receive it to realize that they CAN spend time with Jesus each and every morning—to start their usually "too busy" day . . .

I have to send these early in the morning though, or I won't get them done. Respond to me with a text if you want to continue receiving them and don't worry—you won't hurt my feelings if you don't. If I don't receive a text back, l won't send anymore . . .

The "As per me . . ." part in the middle—are my comments on the writings from others at the start of the devotionals.

Here is today's devotional text . . .

#91. From a brother in Christ . . . in response to a previous early morning devotional text . . .

"Mark, Amen brother! It is a privilege and honor to worship today. Think. Meditate. Read. Pray. Ask. As for me, I'm just trying to cooperate with God's Plan."

As per me . . . in response to him . . . "Great Greg, then you have a proper view of God . . . and are seeing the evidence of His working through you . . . to bear fruit for Him!—AIN'T IT GREAT!!!

As Andrew Murray says in the 12th chapter of his book, *Humility* . . . "There are two stages in the Christian's life . . ."[16] I will paraphrase his statement . . .

The first stage is the preparation stage, in which we are earnestly seeking a relationship with the Lamb of God and ascertaining His will for our lives through time spent communing with Him in prayer and the studying of His Holy Word. The second stage is the fulfillment stage, in which we see Christ, through His Indwelling Holy Spirit . . . using us to impact others and bearing fruit for Him. As well, we encourage them on in their walks of faith, and in their being able to live out that faith!

However, we MUST stay involved in the "preparation"

aspect of our walk of faith daily, hourly, then moment by moment . . . being "immersed" in Christ . . . until we start discovering that Christ Himself is living through us as we die to ourselves—how amazing is our Savior?!

It can all start with 10 minutes each morning . . . right?

Actually, it starts with us each finally being convicted of how sinful we really are . . . and how much we need our Lord Jesus Christ! And then we see our pride . . . melting away—as He helps us to "die to ourselves," and "live for Christ!"—This is when true joy and happiness and meaning for our lives really starts to take place as never before . . . !

"Stay the course" and "stand firm" for our Savior today—sharing Christ and His gospel with those who cross your path . . . TODAY! Jesus Christ has given you life in Him . . . in order to be used by Him, to further His kingdom . . . ! You are THE STEWARD of this life you've been given . . . DON'T SQUANDER IT!!! Don't waste the "PRIVILEGE!" Be Holy . . . !!!

Read utmost.org for Sept. 1st . . . "Destined to be Holy"[17] (a link to the daily devotional *My Utmost for His Highest* by Oswald Chambers)

And He was saying to *them* all, "If anyone wishes to come after Me, let him deny himself, and take up his cross daily, and follow Me. For whoever wishes to save his life shall lose it, but whoever loses his life for My sake, he is the one who will save it."

Luke 9:23-24

Now therefore, O sons, listen to me, for blessed are they who keep my ways. Heed instruction and be wise, and do not neglect *it*. Blessed is the man who listens to me, watching daily at my gates, waiting at my doorposts.

For he who finds me finds life, and obtains favor from the LORD.

Prov. 8:32–35

And the brethren immediately sent Paul and Silas away by night to Berea; and when they arrived, they went into the synagogue of the Jews. Now these were more noble-minded than those in Thessalonica, for they received the word with great eagerness, examining the Scriptures daily, *to see* whether these things were so.

Acts 17:10–11

Now it shall come about when he sits on the throne of his kingdom, he shall write for himself a copy of this law on a scroll in the presence of the Levitical priests. And it shall be with him, and he shall read it all the days of his life, that he may learn to fear the LORD his God, by carefully observing all the words of this law and these statutes, that his heart may not be lifted up above his countrymen and that he may not turn aside from the commandment, to the right or the left; in order that he and his sons may continue long in his kingdom in the midst of Israel.

Deut. 17:18–20

This book of the law shall not depart from your mouth, but you shall meditate on it day and night, so that you may be careful to do according to all that is written in it; for then you will make your way prosperous, and then you will have success. Have I not commanded you? Be strong and courageous! Do not tremble or be dismayed, for the LORD your God is with you wherever you go.

Josh. 1:8–9

"For I know the plans that I have for you," declares the LORD, "plans for welfare and not for calamity to give you a future and a hope. Then you will call upon Me and come and pray to Me, and I will listen to you. And you will seek Me and find *Me*, when you search for Me with all your heart."

Jer. 29:11–13

As obedient children, do not be conformed to the former lusts *which were yours* in your ignorance, but like the Holy One who called you, be holy yourselves also in all *your* behavior; because it is written, "You shall be holy, for I am holy."

1 Pet. 1:14–16

Many of the ones who receive these texts have said that when their cell phone *pings* in the morning, they are compelled to get up and start spending their time with Christ. Here is part of Martyn Lloyd-Jones's spin on "hungering and thirsting after righteousness." Remember that he was speaking this in the 1950s and 1960s:

> The Christian's concern is to view life in this world in the light of the gospel; and, according to the gospel, the trouble with mankind is not any one particular manifestation of sin, but rather sin itself. If you are anxious about the state of the world and the threat of possible wars, then I assure you that the most direct way of avoiding such calamities is to observe words such as these which we are now considering, 'Blessed are they which do hunger and thirst after righteousness: for they shall be filled.' If every man and woman in this world knew what it was to

'hunger and thirst after righteousness' there would be no danger of war. Here is the only way to real peace. All other considerations eventually do not touch the problem, and all the denunciations that are so constantly made of various countries and peoples and persons will not have the slightest effect upon the international situation. Thus, we often waste our time, and God's time, in expressing our human thoughts and sentiments instead of considering His Word. If every human being knew what it was to 'hunger and thirst after righteousness,' the problem would be solved. The greatest need in the world now is for a greater number of Christians, individual Christians. If all nations consisted of individual Christians there would be no need to fear atomic power or anything else. So, the gospel, which seems to be so remote and indirect in its approach, is actually the most direct way of solving the problem. One of the greatest tragedies in the life of the Church today is the way in which so many are content with these vague, general, useless statements about war and peace instead of preaching the gospel in all its simplicity and purity. It is righteousness that exalts a nation, and the most important thing for all of us is to discover what righteousness means.[18]

I am risking here, but I think it is worth doing so. Here is why. This topic and message is VITALLY IMPORTANT to all of us on our walks of faith and it is also the MAJOR DISCONNECT to our growing in our walk of faith with Jesus Christ! Almost everyone I run across is too busy to spend time in prayer, as well as time reading their Bibles. So, what are the chances you are going to read a 585-page book by Martyn Lloyd-Jones on the Sermon on the Mount? I thought so. Do you know why?

There are very few who are even *reading* anything right now. Most people that I visit with about their reading habits tell me that they never read, but that they do watch videos, TV, and movies on their phones and computers! They don't read their Bibles or books by past or present giants in the faith, much less, books on hungering and thirsting for anything that is going to take the effort to spend time reading! So, without printing out the whole book for you, I want to give you some of the insight that I received when reading this giant of a man in the faith's comments. Listen to what Dr. Lloyd-Jones has to say about *happiness* and *hungering and thirsting* implied in this fourth beatitude a couple of pages later:

> The simplest way, perhaps, to approach the text is just to look at its terms. It is one of those texts that divides itself for us, and all we have to do is to look at the meaning of the various terms which are used. Obviously therefore the one to start with is the term 'righteousness.' 'Blessed-or happy-are they which do hunger and thirst after righteousness.' They are the only truly happy people. Now the whole world is seeking for happiness; there is no question about that. Everybody wants to be happy. That is the great motive behind every act and ambition, behind all work and all striving and effort. Everything is designed for happiness. But the great tragedy of the world is that, though it gives itself to seek for happiness, it never seems to be able to find it. The present state of the world reminds us of that very forcibly. What is the matter? I think the answer is that we have never understood this text as we should have done. 'Blessed are they which do hunger and thirst after righteousness.' What does it mean? Let me put it negatively like this. We are not to

hunger and thirst after blessedness; we are not to hunger and thirst after happiness. But that is what most people are doing. We put happiness and blessedness as the one thing that we desire, and thus we always miss it; it always eludes us. According to the Scriptures happiness is never something that should be sought directly; it is always something that results from seeking something else. Now this is true of those outside the Church and of many inside the Church as well. It is obviously the tragedy of those who are outside the Church. The world is seeking for happiness. That is the meaning of its pleasure mania, that is the meaning of everything men and women do, not only in their work but still more in their pleasures. They are trying to find happiness, they are making it their goal, their one objective. But they do not find it because, whenever you put happiness before righteousness, you will be doomed to misery. That is the great message of the Bible from beginning to end. They alone are truly happy who are seeking to be righteous. Put happiness in the place of righteousness and you will never get it.[19]

This explains much of what we see around us each and every day. All of those stars in Hollywood, all the rich and famous, all of those who seemingly *have it made* in the world. What eludes them? Happiness eludes them—because they are all seeking happiness in all the wrong places. There is only one place where that happiness can be found, and it is in the joy of being "in Christ!"

But the one who joins himself to the Lord is one spirit *with Him*. Flee immorality. Every *other* sin that a man commits is outside the body, but the immoral man sins

against his own body. Or do you not know that your
body is a temple of the Holy Spirit who is in you, whom
you have from God, and that you are not your own? For
you have been bought with a price: therefore glorify
God in your body.

1 Cor. 6:17–20

I say, "Amen to this!" because I am finding that I am living
it out after all these years of seeking my own happiness in all
the wrong places. Why on earth did it take me so very long?
It was my self-centered pride that was getting in my way for
all *my* seeking for *my* happiness. As the Lord has given me the
desire and persistence to seek Him out more and more, I find
that my concern for myself is diminishing while my seeking
Christ takes a turn towards Him just like I'm being drawn like
a magnet—to Him! The more closely I avail myself to Jesus and
His trait of being a *servant* of love and compassion to others, the
happier and more content my life has become. I am seeing Jesus
do things in and through my life that He has given me—in spite
of myself and my sins that I still commit!

I am realizing that each day is an ADVENTURE! And the
Lord is working all around me throughout each day. He has
opened my eyes to enable me to see those who are hurting
with their own heartaches, and then to reach out to them and
comfort them with the *love of Christ*. I find myself praying
more and more with people at my practice and on the phone.
The Holy Spirit is giving me more of a *servant* heart as opposed
to a *being served* heart. He is helping me to become more of
a disciple for Him. And not only that, Jesus is helping me to
have the extremely fulfilling joy of encouraging others around
me to help them become disciples as well. After all, that is a
lot of what the Lord wants us to do. Not only does He want
us to share His gospel with those we come in contact with,

but He wants us to *be disciples* and then to *make disciples*! We will not find ourselves on this path if we are not *hungering and thirsting for Christ's righteousness* each day. We must have a daily relationship with Jesus Christ! Only then will we find that the daily relationship turns into a resultant moment-by-moment relationship!

What is each of us doing with the *gift* of each day that we are given? Will we also waste this one TODAY???

CHAPTER 5

!

Nevertheless you will die like men and fall like any one
of the princes. Arise, O God, judge the earth! For it is
You who possesses all the nations.

Ps. 82:7–8

I've had a couple of people comment on my using the
exclamation point to head up this chapter. Here is the
reasoning. The Lord started me off using this structure for the
chapters of the first and the second book, so it seemed only
proper to do so for this third book as the title evolved. But
there is more to it than that. What do you see when you see
an exclamation point? I see an emphasis . . . or an urgency
to the statement that was made before. This is why I'm using
it in the title of *If You Die Today!* It implies that the title
has an *urgency* to it! That urgency is there because death is
coming to each of us one day, and it could come today for any
one of us!

We each don't know when, but *death* IS coming—for each
of us! Death had shown its first shadow to my own immediate
family, and it was resting on my mother. She had called a day
or two before to let us know, and my big brother, Frank, and

I headed up on the long drive to west Texas. Our sister, Mary Beth, who's an RN, was also meeting us there. Frank and I were about halfway there when I thought it was as good a time as any to pose the question: "Frank, if you die today, where will you be tomorrow?"

His answer was a little of a surprise, but in reflection now, why should it have been?

"I don't know," was the reply that came across the front seat of the car.

I had heard that same answer from my Dad not too long before.

My response was pretty quick, but not brash. "Well, Frank, I know where I would be. I'd be with Jesus Christ and all the saints for eternity, and I want you to be there as well."

I let it stop there and sink in for the rest of the trip. We will pick up on my brother later.

We Each Have an Unalterable Appointment!

"It is written in the book"—this is the comment that one of our family friends has made repeatedly to Keyea. It is her way of saying that none of us knows when or how we are going to die— it is written in God's book and His plan.

Right now, I would like to speak to you about the special lady my brother and I were on the way to check on, my mom, Grace. She and Dad had been married 49 years, and it was the only marriage either of them ever had. When we arrived at the hospital, I could tell this wasn't a good situation. The concerned and somber look on Dad's face explained it all. It was a bad and serious diagnosis. The tests and scans revealed the lung cancer that would eventually take our mother's life, but with chemo-treatments and radiation therapy, her time with us would be extended. The original prognosis was eight to nine months, but she lived for another 26 months, so we had over two years to say goodbye. That was the kind of fighter she was.

Our mother was a strong lady who devoted herself to helping her husband, kids, and anyone else she could. At times, we each felt that maybe she was offering too much advice, but her guidance was usually incredibly spot-on! With her diagnosis came the realization that although she was a hard charger, even she was fallible. Sixteen years since she passed, her legacy of love and service is a lesson that follows me even still. Not one time during her illness did my mom question the Lord about her cancer and impending death, nor did she show any resentment or anger toward Christ. I remember her telling me while she and I sat on the driveway in front of the garage door, her floppy hat covering her hairless head, "You know, Mark, the Lord has blessed our family so very much; and I am so thankful for your dad and you kids, with your families! I've lived such a blessed life, and I love you all so much, *shug*!" My mother was a beautiful lady inside and out, but never had she been more beautiful to me than at that moment.

She faced death as the woman of faith, integrity, and strength she was, carried by the stronger Savior she worshiped. Her unquestioning faith in Jesus Christ was an example, as well as a *gift*, that will always be with me for eternity. I know now that I took for granted her love and concern for me throughout my life. I also know that her life so impacted me that it has helped lead to the writing of these books and my sharing of my faith with others—whether they wanted to hear it or not! I'm a lot like her on the giving of advice to others. I love and miss her dearly, but look forward to reuniting with her some day for eternity!

I solemnly charge *you* in the presence of God and of Christ Jesus, who is to judge the living and the dead, and by His appearing and His kingdom: preach the

word; be ready in season *and* out of season; reprove, rebuke, exhort, with great patience and instruction. For the time will come when they will not endure sound doctrine; but *wanting* to have their ears tickled, they will accumulate for themselves teachers in accordance to their own desires; and will turn away their ears from the truth, and will turn aside to myths. But you, be sober in all things, endure hardship, do the work of an evangelist, fulfill your ministry.

2 Tim. 4:1–5

We each have a job to do and a ministry to fulfill. That ministry includes being a light to those around us about the truth of the gospel of Jesus Christ. We were fortunate in Mother's case that she had a strong faith in our Savior before her diagnosis. There are many around us who don't have that same faith, but they do have this unalterable appointment with death. After all, "it is written in the book!" We, however, seem to do just as I did with my mother: we take it for granted that they are prepared for the worst-case scenario about their own lives. We shouldn't do that. We could all do a better job at helping those around us to take more steps on their walks of faith before they are impacted by traumatic events that are sure to come into their lives.

Our taking things for granted goes on in our own walks of faith with Jesus our Savior as well. Would you not agree? Our disciplined and persistent relationship with Jesus is a difficult endeavor for all of us—especially with the right heart motive and with an eagerness to hunger and thirst after His righteousness. The main way the Lord is able to transform our sinful and depraved hearts and minds (Rom. 12:1–2) is through our spending time with Him in relationship, in prayer, and in His living Word. But time is hard to come by, is it not? I am thankful that the Lord has enabled me to get that habit formed some 34 years ago now. Yes, discipline and persistence are good, but somewhere in the mix, the right motive must come to the fore. Spending time in prayer and His Word is worthless if we do so only to check off a box for our own pride to share with others. What I have found, however, was that by committing to that time each morning, my heart and mind are being transformed. The Lord has changed my priorities, goals, and purpose for living!

The Phone Call That Could Have Been Missed . . .

When I got a call at my office one Friday afternoon, the Lord was able to have me ready! First, you must understand that I am never at my office on a Friday afternoon. Dentistry is too stressful to do it more than four days per week. (Kidding.) But really, I am never in my office on a Friday afternoon, and this was when landlines were still the order of the day. For some bewildering reason, I was in the laboratory of my office taking care of a case that had to be ready to go out Monday morning. I think I was flying down to teach in Florida that next week, so I had to get it ready. You can imagine how surprised I was when my phone in the lab rang and it was my brother, Frank, on the other end.

"Hey, what's up?" he stated.

"Not much, just tying up some loose ends getting ready to head to Miami."

"Oh, okay. Hey, I've got a question for you. I got an email from a friend. It's a Bible verse that has me confused."

"Which verse?" I asked.

"Revelation 2:16–17. It says, '**Therefore repent; or else I am coming to you quickly, and I will make war against them with the sword of My mouth. He who has an ear, let him hear**

what the Spirit says to the churches. To him who overcomes, to him I will give *some* **of the hidden manna, and I will give him a white stone, and a new name written on the stone which no one knows but he who receives it.'** So, what is this all about?"

"Frank, that is speaking of the second coming of Jesus Christ, when He returns to the earth to judge the people of the earth. At that, or some juncture, there will be no changing of minds for those who have refused to receive Jesus as their Savior, and those who refuse Him will be condemned to hell for eternity— with no possible chance to come back to Him! The die is cast and they will be lost in hell forever!"

"Well that sounds pretty tough! When is that going to happen?"

"No one knows, Frank. It could happen at any time. It could happen today!"

"Really."

"Yes, really! Would you like to know that you would be with Jesus Christ and the saints in heaven for eternity? You know, if you do, we could settle this on the phone right here right now."

"How?"

"You could acknowledge that you are a sinner, repent of your sins, and receive Jesus Christ as your Lord and Savior on this phone right now—and have the assurance that Christ will hear you, and you will be in heaven for eternity. Would you like to do that—now?"

"Yes, I would."

"Frank, let's pray . . ."

My big brother repented of his sin and received Jesus Christ as his Lord right there on the phone that Friday afternoon— when I am never normally in my office! Isn't it amazing that God orchestrates our lives and gives us opportunities each and every day to further His kingdom? The question is always there for us. Will we be tuned in to our Savior, to those who are lost around us, and to where they will spend eternity? If we are focused on these three aspects of the truth that surround us each day, we will see rampant and endless opportunities to serve our God and those He sends our way! Each day will be filled with purposeful intent! It will be so because we will be seeing with new eyes opened to the heartache and desperate searching for hope in the glazed-over eyes of those we meet. What has your attention and focus the most?

Oh, and by the way, my big brother is still doing well in his walk of faith. His growth and maturing in Jesus Christ is something to behold. He is actively sharing with others the gospel of Jesus Christ and inviting them to go to Bible study with him. Not only is he growing in his faith, but he is helping me to grow in mine and others around him to grow in theirs! Isn't it amazing the way the Lord can use us sinners, even in spite of ourselves?

"Mark, I'm feeling terrible and am going to the ER!"

It was my best friend over the last 35 years on the other end of the phone. He lived in a suburb of Chicago called Arlington Heights. Mike and I met at a post-graduate dental Institute down in Miami in 1980. What had started as a chance meeting grew into a brotherly friendship that consisted of 22 years of yearly get-togethers until kids and busyness got in the way. We maintained 35 years of friendship with long phone conversations every one or two weeks. Living so far apart gave us the opportunity to share things some might not as readily share in a closer proximity. We knew one another's practices, incomes, and dreams for our careers and family. And yes, we knew a lot about one another's difficulties and trials in staying the course in our walks of faith with our Savior. We were growing in our faith, but not as much as we would have liked. Both of us were in reasonably good health all through these years.

That was partly why I was surprised when he had his spleen removed just a couple of summers ago. He had been having soreness and shortness of breath when he and Cindy were walking and jogging together. The surgery went well, and the biopsy proved that the spleen situation was benign—which is a good thing. That surgery was in August 2015.

But six months later, here Mike was, calling me and sharing that he was going to the ER. This time the pain was different and even more intense than before. I told him to get to the hospital and let me know what they found out. The call later from his wife, Cindy, was somber. It took two weeks for them to determine the cause was cancer, and they gave him 6–18 months to live, although they didn't know what type of cancer it was.

All this had happened so fast. Mike had been in such good health the month previous when he gave the Mayor's Prayer Breakfast address in Arlington Heights.[20] His talk to the 250 people present spoke of his commitment to Jesus Christ and his recommitment to spend more time with Cindy and his kids—time he wished he had spent earlier in his life instead of chasing his dreams for his success. But now, about a month after the talk, he had hardly a year projected for his life.

Six weeks later, still with no definitive diagnosis, Cindy called and asked if she and Mike could FaceTime with me. The image on the other end of the phone grabbed me by the throat, and I could hardly get any words out! When I got home that evening, I told Keyea that I had to get to Chicago, quickly! I've got a great wife. She told me to "get after it," knowing I should go. When I arrived at Mike's hospital room that Friday, he cleared the room of visitors except for Cindy and me. He looked at me, then at Cindy, and back.

"Mark, Cindy and I are determined that whatever happens in relation to this diagnosis, we want it to be glorifying to the Lord. He alone is in control, and we are good with whichever direction Jesus takes this. I know where I am going, and so does Cindy—may His will be done."

Later that day, Mike told me that he had a favor to ask of me: "Would you help me present the gospel to my three brothers and my three buddies from my childhood? I just want to make sure that they hear it from me and you, so they have the opportunity to receive Jesus Christ. Also, I would like Nate and Jake [his sons] to be in the room to hear it."

"That's not a problem, Mike. I'm all over that. We will make that happen." And we did!

That Sunday morning when I went in to say goodbye to Mike, it was one of the hardest things I've ever done in my life! I knew this would be the last time I would lay eyes on him this side of heaven. The 1- to 2-week interval phone calls we made to one another for those 35 years would be at an end. He and I each picking up the phone when we knew it was the other on the line and saying, "Hel-lo!" would not happen one more time. The laughing at both of our strengths and weaknesses together on the phone would be missed—a LOT!

Cindy took a picture of us while we were all smiles and saying "Bye" to one another. I told him I loved him and would see him soon! He replied with the same! I leaned over his hospital bed and gave him one last hug as he squeezed me all he could in his weakened state, "I love you, Mark!"

"I love you so much, Mike!"

I shot him a smile when I left while he did the same back. I walked out into the hall of the hospital with Cindy and I made it about 15 feet down the hall and stopped . . . She could see the tears welling up in my eyes as I saw her doing the same. I don't know that I've ever wept that uncontrollably in my life . . . !

Here is the picture Cindy took.

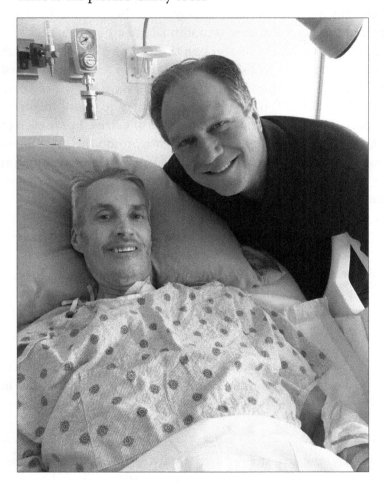

Mike died three weeks later, on Mother's Day 2016. Cindy asked if I would come back and speak at Mike's funeral. It was an honor I would not have even thought of passing up. There were between 800–1,000 people at Mike's visitation and probably between 500–600 at his funeral. This was one of those times that the Lord has given me to have an opportunity to be nothing but a servant! Jesus gave me opportunities to serve both the weekend I went to stay with them at the hospital, and at the funeral almost a month later, and I am so thankful that I didn't miss them. Through those two visits, the Lord has accomplished much in training me up and teaching me what it means to serve those who are losing or have lost a loved one. This is a difficult, but rewarding ministry to those involved, especially when it is bathed in the love of Christ. I pray each of you will use your ability through Christ to do the same when you are given the chance. It grew me a tremendous amount in my walk of faith, but too, it gave me a chance to show unconditional love!

We have come to know and have believed the love which God has for us. God is love, and the one who abides in love abides in God, and God abides in him. By this, love is perfected with us, that we may have confidence in the day of judgment; because as He is, so also are we in this world.

1 John 4:16–17

Listen to what Martyn Lloyd-Jones says in his book, *Life in Christ: Studies in 1 John*, where he writes this in the chapter entitled "Dwelling in Love":

But let me go a step further and put it like this: The great characteristic of the love of God, therefore, is that God does not consider Himself—God does not consider His own honour and glory. Rather, God considers us. God as He looks upon us does not go on saying, 'This is what

they have done to Me, this is how they have behaved with
respect to Me—they have rebelled against Me; they have
become offensive, ugly, and foul as the result of their
attitude, and therefore . . . ' Not at all! God – I say it again
with reverence—in His dealings with us in Christ has not
been considering Himself. He has considered us and our
lost condition, and it is for that reason that He has done
what He has done.

'So if we are Christians,' says John in effect, 'it means that
God is in us, and God is love; therefore, we must be like
that.' That means our attitude must not be determined
and controlled by what other people are like or by what
they do. It also does not mean that we are always to save
ourselves and to claim the right of justice and honour and
credit all these other things. It means that we are not to
look at ourselves and what we are doing; it means that we
are to look at others and forget self in this extraordinary
way and manner.

In other words, we can go a step further and put it like
this: it means that, like God, we must see others as souls.
We must see their need and their sorry plight; we must
see them as victims of sin and of Satan. These things need
no demonstration; there would not have been a single
Christian were this not true of God. God looked upon us
and the world, and He did not see us; He saw, rather, our
captivity to Satan. He saw us in the bondage of iniquity;
He saw that we were being ruined by this evil thing. He
looked at us in spite of our sin; and as He is, so must we
be if He is in us. 'As He is, so are we in this world'; and
that means, of course that having looked upon others,

> not just as they are in all their offensiveness and in all their difficulty, we see them rather as lost souls. We see them as the serfs of Satan, as the victims of these evil powers and wickednesses in the heavenly places, and we are sorry for them, and compassion enters into our heart for them.[21]

Lloyd-Jones goes on to say:

> The result is that as God is in us, so we become ready to forgive and to forget, for that is what God has done with us. God has looked upon us and forgiven us; and even more wonderful, He has forgotten our sins – He has cast our sins into the sea of His forgetfulness. What a loving, wonderful thought that is, that God not only forgives our sin, but He has forgotten all about it! Only Omnipotence can do that. Thank God He can! He does not remember my past sins; He has forgotten them and they are gone. Psalm 103:12—"As far as the east is from the west, So far has He removed our transgressions from us." Blessed be His name![22]

Regarding death, love, forgiving and forgetting our sins Lloyd-Jones states:

> "God was active and did something—He sent His Son, in spite of it all, into the world."[23]

Have this attitude in yourselves which was also in Christ Jesus, who, although He existed in the form of God, did not regard equality with God a thing to be grasped, but emptied Himself, taking the form of a

bond-servant, *and* being made in the likeness of men. Being found in appearance as a man, He humbled Himself by becoming obedient to the point of death, even death on a cross.

Phil. 2:5–8

Lloyd-Jones then says the following:

God the Father and God the Son spoke together in the eternal council about men and women in their lost state and condition and in their need of salvation. And when the Father laid the problem before the Son and asked Him, 'Are You ready to do it?' He did not say, 'Am I to forsake heaven? Am I to humble myself? Is it fair? I am equal with You!' No! He 'thought it not robbery to be equal with God,' but that did not make Him prize and clutch at the heavenly glories. He gladly put it all to one side; He divested Himself of the insignia of His eternal glory. He humbled Himself, took upon Him the form of a servant, and faced the death of the cross, never thinking of Himself.[24]

Should we, as followers of Christ, not be doing the same thing for Him and for those around us? If Christ is dwelling in us through His Holy Spirit, should we not be denying ourselves and showing His love to all of those around us, no matter the circumstances?

And He was saying to *them* all, "If anyone wishes to come after Me, let him deny himself, and take up his cross daily, and follow Me. For whoever wishes to save his life shall lose it, but whoever loses his life for My sake, he is the one who will save it. For what is a

man profited if he gains the whole world, and loses or
forfeits himself? For whoever is ashamed of Me and My
words, the Son of Man will be ashamed of him when He
comes in His glory, and *the glory* of the Father and of
the holy angels.

Luke 9:23–26

Are any of us truly denying ourselves, taking up our crosses,
and following Jesus?

Or are we ashamed of Christ? These are questions most of us
spend little time pondering in our self-serving and busy world.
Might it be good for us to each take time to do so and examine
ourselves and our relationship with Christ?

It Took 15 Minutes . . . Maybe 20 at the Max!

Keyea and I were driving home one night from one of our
weekly dinner dates. As we drove, I couldn't help but think
about my patient, Ernie. He was probably one mile away, lying
in his Intensive Care hospital bed. Pulling up to the traffic light
on the way home, a few minutes later, I asked, "Keyea, would
you mind if I stopped to visit with a patient in the hospital for
a few minutes?"

"Go for it!"

Keyea stayed in the car while I entered and asked the nurses
which room he was in. When I got there, his daughter greeted
me.

"My name is Mark, and I'm Ernie's dentist."

"Oh, OK. Thank you for coming," she said with a look of
genuine appreciation.

Since he was asleep, she and I quietly talked about his health.
He was in a tough battle for his life with complex issues to deal
with. I was just getting ready to step out the door when he

coughed and opened his eyes for a few seconds. He caught a glimpse of me and coughed again, focusing more intently.

"Mark! Thanks for coming!" he said with more force than I thought he would be able to muster in his present state.

I walked around his bed to the other side and leaned down to be within a couple of feet, face-to-face. "Hey man! You're looking good, Ernie! I thought I would stop by and check on you tonight. How're you feeling?"

"I've been better, but I have improved some over the last few days."

"Ernie, would you mind if I prayed for you right now?"

"No! In fact, Mark, I was hoping you would do that."

Ernie, his daughter, and I clasped our hands together above his chest, and I prayed for him. You would not believe the gratitude in his eyes when we had finished.

"Mark, I so appreciate you coming by to visit me!" he said as the nurse came in to take his vitals.

"Not a problem, Ernie! Give me your cell number, and I'll send you a devotional text I send out each morning. And you can text or call me anytime."

I got out of the way and let the nurse get on with her duties. I told his daughter to call or text me if I could help in any way. It took all of 15–20 minutes, but I know that to Ernie and his family, it was huge to have someone stop by and pray with them! Why do we not show the love of Christ more in caring for those around us? We must be in tune with our Lord and with those He has brought across our path, and then show them the love of Christ.

The shadow of death has rested on some of these people that I have related in this chapter, but don't let us fool ourselves: the urgency of death will come and will rest on each one of us one day! Our time is written in the book!

CHAPTER 6

WHERE

Again there was a day when the sons of God came to present themselves before the LORD, and Satan also came among them to present himself before the LORD. And the LORD said to Satan, "Where have you come from?" Then Satan answered the LORD and said, "From roaming about on the earth, and walking around on it."

Job 2:1–2

Where will we each end up? I know we are here on this earth for right now, but where will we be when our lives are spent, and we have passed through that doorway of death? We haven't been to that place yet, so we either try to ignore it and say it is never coming, or discount that it is even in our future. There are three possibilities, right? One is that we will be dead and gone with no eternal life anywhere. Or we will be in one of two places the Bible speaks of—heaven or hell. Which of these scenarios do you think is the reality of where you will be?

"Mark, I see no light at the end of the tunnel . . ."

Dennis has been a patient of mine for about 25 years, maybe more. He is a self-made man whose entrepreneurial spirit is alive and well, as evidenced by his passion for technology and his flair for carrying his business to an international market. We have mainly had conversations about his business dealings and hunting exploits through the years. This morning was different. Hurricane Harvey had just trudged through south Texas, covering the greater Houston area with massive and catastrophic flooding. I had tried to get the computer up and running at the office on Monday, but couldn't retrieve the schedule to call and tell people not to bother coming in. The ladies at the office were game to come in on Tuesday morning and get in touch with patients, and sure enough, Dennis showed up promptly at 8:00 a.m. for his cleaning visit. Because there was no one else coming in for an appointment with all the flooding going on, after his cleaning, he and I sat in my private office to visit, as I do with so many of my patients. I asked him where his next hunt was and how his business was doing, so he filled me in on both.

Then, out of the blue he said, "You know, Mark, I just don't get it. Where do you get the time to write these books you've written? I noticed them sitting out on the counter again as I walked in this morning. You know, I see that as a monumental undertaking—to think about getting a book to print. How do you find the time to do so?"

"I didn't ever intend to write any books, Dennis. It wasn't my idea."

"What do you mean?"

"I really mean that: I had no aspirations or inklings that I would ever write one book, much less three."

"I thought you had written two books."

"I have, but I'm working on the third."

"Really, what is it about?"

"Dennis, I know that we haven't discussed this any, but I think you know my faith is very important to me. This third book is connected to the two before it: it speaks to our faith or lack of it. But I realize that not everyone is comfortable in talking about this subject. It is a very private issue for so many."

"It is funny that you should mention this, Mark, because I have been thinking about this topic a pretty good bit here lately. I know that your faith is important to you and that you don't want to offend me, but I want you to realize something else— I'm open to talking about this with you. I'd like to hear what you have to say to me about your faith. I can see that it is an important part of your life."

"That's great, Dennis; I'd be happy to. For years, I've been asking a question of people and the answers they have given have been very diverse. I want to be a stepping stone and not a stumbling block to people and help them to understand that I'm not judging them, but that I want to help them think about what they are doing with their lives. Do you mind if I ask you this same question? It is kind of personal."

"I really am comfortable and open to visiting with you about this. Let me hear it."

"Dennis, if you die today, where will you be tomorrow?"

"I'll be in a box," he said.

"Do you know, I've had several others tell me that they would be in the morgue, in the ground, six feet under—very similar answers to what you've said. It is interesting to see how people respond."

"Well, since I was in college, I've been rolling this story

about Jesus around and around in my head, and I just don't buy it. I'm 79 years old now, and I'm getting to the end of the tunnel of my life, and I just don't see any light at the end of it."

"I understand that. I was at a similar place when I got out of college. I'm not sure I really bought it back then either. It is interesting that you brought up the "box" though—what if you're mistaken? What if you are not just dead, gone, and stuffed in that box? What concerns me is that the choice we each make today regarding our faith, will impact where we spend eternity, if there is one. And if there is, I hate to think of people spending eternity separated from God and in a terrible place of torment and agony—forever!"

"You know, that's why I think all this has been weighing on me here of late. I'm getting closer to the end of my life and what if I'm wrong about eternity?" he said.

"Dennis, I was once asked to give a talk on my Christian faith at the junior college down south of here to a World Religion Class. There were numerous other people speaking for various other faiths as well. I titled my presentation "Place Your Bets" because I think that is what all of us are doing. The Hindus are placing their bets on the millions of gods they worship, the Buddhists . . . Buddha, the Muslims . . . Allah; atheists are even placing their bets that none of it is true because they believe there is no eternity and no life after death. They will not all be right, will they? I'm convinced that God's plan of redemption is the only one that truly makes sense. And even it doesn't make sense as many first think about it. Once they do contemplate it, many find that God's ultimate plan of redemption of sinful man is the only one that does seem to make sense. Many, myself included, find the more we spend time in His Word and in prayer, God's plan begins to unfold, and He shows us that His plan is PERFECT! Think about God's plan. God the Father sends His Son, Jesus Christ, to come down to earth from heaven to be born of a virgin, take on human flesh, and live a perfectly sinless life that none of us sinners could possibly live. Then that same Son, Who performed all those many miracles, goes willingly to die on the cross to pay the penalty for your sins and mine, which you or I could never possibly pay the price for. And not only does He shed His blood and die on the cross to atone for our sins, but He is buried in the tomb for three days and then rises again, bodily appearing to more than 500 people on numerous occasions. Jesus Christ's doing all this and ascending into heaven having paid the price for our sins enables us to be saved by Him from those sins and from death. We can believe in Him as our Lord and receive His loving atonement for our sins, which saves us from God's wrath which will someday be meted out on all the world's sins! All of this just doesn't make sense. But God did so anyway, because it is His ultimate and perfect plan for redeeming those in sinful mankind who turn their lives over to His Son in faith!"

"I haven't heard it quite put that way, Mark, and I want you to know how much I appreciate you taking the time to visit with me about this."

"I'm going to give you my books, if you'll take them, Dennis. Also, I'll give you this printout of the Place Your Bets presentation I gave. You may find it helpful."

"Technical reading is almost all of what I usually read. However, I'm going to assure you that I am now going to read all this you are giving me. You've peaked my interest."

"Great! I hope you have a great hunting trip and if you ever have any questions about any of this, feel free to give me a call. I'm available."

"Will do . . . and I would like to visit about all of this with you again sometime. Like I said, I am open," as he took everything I gave him and walked out of the office.

Place Your Bets!

We will not know exactly where we will be until we are there—the moment after we each die. But the three alternatives that I mentioned before seem to be the most feasible—either there is a heaven and a hell, or there is nothing. That there is no eternity is a bet, which possibly most people in the world have, based on how they are living out their lives. There are many who would say there is a heaven, but many surveys indicate that fewer people think that an actual hell exists. Are we just exercising wishful thinking here, or are we really interested in determining the truth?

When you get right down to it, most in our world now would seem to fit in the category that ascribe to the belief that there is no absolute truth. Therefore, they say the Bible is not all true, God is not all true, nor are the sciences. This is how we get to this place we seem to be in our world now where we literally have no definitive right or wrong out there. Individuals can think they are a man one day of the week, and then decide they are a woman the next. This then enables them to decide which bathroom they feel like going in to use that day. Did you ever think we would get to this level of insanity? I sure didn't! We could stay on this merry-go-round for the rest of our lives and get to no real discussion of the issue of eternity, so I am going to make an executive decision here—after all, this book is intended to be a possible help for us all to get to the one truth—God's truth. After spending 34 years studying God's Holy Word and experiencing that it is absolutely true, I am going to take a stand that I have taken for decades: God's Word is the absolute truth! As is Jesus Christ! Jesus says so Himself when He is being questioned by Pilate, before His crucifixion:

> **Jesus answered, "My kingdom is not of this world. If My kingdom were of this world, then My servants would be fighting so that I might not be delivered up to the Jews; but as it is, my kingdom is not of this realm." Therefore Pilate said to Him, "So You are a king?" Jesus answered, "You say *correctly* that I am a king. For this I have been born, and for this I have come into the world, to testify to the truth. Everyone who is of the truth hears My voice." Pilate said to Him, "What is truth?" And when he had said this, he went out again to the Jews, and said to them, "I find no guilt in Him.**
> **John 18:36–38**

Jesus was sent by His Father to come into the world to bear witness to the truth! The sharing of this truth is something that should be one of the top priorities for all of us who are believers in Jesus Christ. It was with this in mind, that I accepted that invitation to share my faith at the World Religion Class at the Junior College. The "Place Your Bets" PowerPoint presentation I gave has lent itself to my having it printed up in pamphlet form to hand out to patients who have questions about what the gospel message of Christianity is. Here it is as it appears on each page of the pamphlet:

Page 1 – Place Your Bets by Mark Peters (the title page)

Page 2 – Rhetorical Questions . . .

- Do you believe that there is a heaven?
- Do you believe there is a hell?

- Do you want to spend eternity in heaven?
- If you die today, where will you be tomorrow?
- Why would you be there?
- Are you sure?
- Is there such a thing as absolute truth?
- Do you believe it?
- Do all roads of faith lead to heaven?

Page 3 – My Testimony . . .

- I was in church sporadically until the 9th grade; then I stopped altogether.
- I truly don't believe I received Jesus Christ as my Lord until I was 28 years old—when a dentist I was working with invited me to a Christian concert.
- He then gave Keyea and me a Bible, which I didn't read!
- A year later, a friend told me not to read Revelation, because it would scare the heck out of me. When I got home, I did—and he was right!
- I discovered I didn't know the Lord I said I worshiped!!!
- The Lord put it on my heart to spend time in prayer and in His Word each day about 34 years ago.
- I'm now in my 29th year in BSF (Bible Study Fellowship).
- My wife, daughter, son, and I have over 84 cumulative years in BSF between the four of us.

- Besides Bible study each day, I've read over 4,300 pages of Charles Haddon Spurgeon's sermons, as well as many books on the Christian faith.

- Though some would say I've been diligent in earnestly seeking our Lord and being the spiritual leader of my family—I know that I still fall far short and am a depraved sinner and have no righteousness of my own!

Page 4 – The gospel message

1. God is perfect and His righteous and perfect holiness is the standard for all who will be in heaven.

2. We are all born into sin and thus are separated from the Holy God.

3. God sent his son Jesus Christ to take on human flesh, live a perfectly sinless life, and offer Himself as the perfect sacrifice for all those who believe in Him as their Lord and Savior and only hope.

4. When we repent of our sin and receive Jesus Christ as our Lord and Savior in faith, our sins past, present, and future are imputed onto Him on the cross on which He shed his blood as an atonement and gave His life as a ransom for believers, and we are sealed with the Holy Spirit for eternity.

5. As believers in Jesus Christ, we are clothed in Christ's righteousness and made holy through His perfect sacrifice on the cross, not through any effort of our own.

6. As believers, through the indwelling Holy Spirit, we are enabled to participate in God's perfect plan of redemption . . . or not!

- Have you written down what you believe in?

- My life purpose (revealed to me in prayer in 1990 and revised in 2017): "I am here to serve my Lord Who sent me, to serve those He sends to me, with reverence, humility, and the love of Christ—all for His glory."

- What are we doing with our walks of faith while we are living on this earth?

- We are . . .

Page 5 – "Placing Our Bets . . ." (on the full page)

Page 6 – What I believe . . .

- I believe in the Triune God—God the Father, God the Son, and God the Holy Spirit, all separate but equally One, each eternal **(Eph. 2:17–18, Gal. 4:6, Gen. 1:1–2, John 1:1–14).**

- I believe that the Bible is the holy and inspired, living Word of God Who loves us **(2 Tim. 3:16–17).**

- I believe that every person born on this earth is born with a sin nature . . . which deserves the wrath of God's judgment; none of us are righteous or good **(Eph. 2:1–3, Isa. 64:6, Rom. 3:10–12).**

- I believe that Jesus Christ was the only one not born into sin. He was 100% God and 100% man. Jesus was conceived of the Holy Spirit, born of the virgin Mary, was crucified dead and buried. The third day He arose from the dead, was resurrected, and sits at the right hand of God the Father in heaven (**Isa. 7:14, Matt. 1:23, Heb. 4:15, Matt. 22:44**).

- I BELIEVE THAT Jesus Christ lived a perfect and sinless life, and though He was tempted in every way we are . . . He was always obedient to do the will of His Father in heaven (**Heb. 5:9, Heb. 4:15, Heb. 9:11**).

- I believe that Jesus Christ's perfect and atoning sacrifice on the cross, as well as His death and resurrection . . . made the way for the forgiveness of sins and subsequent indwelling of the Holy Spirit to be given into the hearts of believers for their sanctification and for the furthering of God's kingdom . . . for his glory (**2 Cor. 5:17–21, Rom. 3:20–31**).

Page 7 – Self-sacrifice . . .

- "Self-sacrifice" is a quality many people admire but may not really want to practice. Modern culture expects self-interest, which is natural to all of us.

- Even when committing to serve God and other people, we may struggle with thoughts that silently ask, "What is in this for me?"

- Jesus Christ was the most sacrificial man who ever lived. He gave everything. Because of that, we can live forever with Him as we believe in Him.

- He also called His people to follow Him in self-denial and sacrifice. This command does not earn forgiveness of sin nor a place in God's family.